A COOKBOOK FOR POOR POETS
(AND OTHERS)

A COOKBOOK
for POOR POETS
(and others)

by Ann Rogers

Charles Scribner's Sons · New York

CONTENTS

FOREWORD

Poets are often out of funds. Many times they try to keep body and soul together by eating candy bars, apples, doughnuts, and an occasional hamburger, usually standing up. This is a mistake. Meals should be eaten sitting down.

This book will be devoted to sitting-down meals, however humble. It will try to deal with food, however simple and inexpensive, which makes some appeal not only to taste but to sight, touch, smell, and (occasionally) hearing. Some meals will not need the aid of fire (for it is sometimes too expensive or out of reach). Others will. The simplicities of custom will sometimes be called upon; the conveniences of modern processing will also come into view.

The author realizes that other people than poets are sometimes very hard up indeed. These others (young wives and husbands making ends meet, students, musicians with uncopied scores and painters with unsold pictures, novelists in the middle of a novel, older people with small fixed stipends, and people who like to work only occasionally) may well benefit from the good sense of the following suggestions. They are offered with warm sympathy, from the wide experience of Miss Rogers and Miss Rogers' family —born and inventive cooks all.

LOUISE BOGAN

March, 1965

A COOKBOOK FOR POOR POETS
(AND OTHERS)

INTRODUCTION

The nickel dinner would, in periods of poverty, be gratifying indeed. Then, during those too chance bonanza moments, the same dinner could be a manifold blessing—not the least of which would be a coin or two toward the next private depression, whether it be prefaced by purchase of a painting too dear, three bars of imported soap, a box of strawberries out of season, or an unexpected tonsillectomy.

Yes, if there were truly a nickel dinner. But one can come close to this goal, not with a candy bar (for a candy bar is not really dinner) but with a big fresh roll—the French or Italian kind—the crust shattering with the first bite, the inside a network of intricate passages and domed rooms! It smells of yeast and wheatfields and waterfalls and salt flats. And because its very texture requires slow and careful munching, and each crumb must be picked up, it provides time for these natural, fragrant associations.

So this is the first rule: always have fresh bread.

The second is: always use butter.

In one period of poverty advisers noted that butter was an extravagance and that *no one* bought it. Except, perhaps, the sculptors in India who carve statues from it. Mulling over this bit of economic lore, I decided right then that I, forthwith, would always cook with butter.

The third rule: always serve wine.

There are educationally sterile methods for teaching children the days of the week. I learned Sunday first, for this was the day to go with father to buy the wine.

We brought a big empty jug and went through the Italian grocer's to the cool dim back room that was pungent with lees and oak. And over it all, the dry mustiness of vineyards in sunshine.

This was during the depression, and Sunday dinners were sometimes meager. Often they had to be stretched for friends.

But they were always gala. There was always wine. And there was always fresh bread and butter. It was, in a way, truly a nickel dinner.

And as the depression slowly receded, so does the need for the nickel dinner. For one day there is not a rejection slip nor the refusal of a job, but a check. A small check—for it is, after all, a very small first effort.

It is now time to celebrate and to expand the menu. Or perhaps, to lay in a little store of staples.

. . .

Staples are not necessarily a sack of flour and a box of salt. Staples are whatever it is that makes the Poor Poet, and others who cook, feel secure.

There is one who says, "When I come back from Chinatown with a sack of rice, I feel secure." And another thinks, "If I had a supply of dried beans— enough to last all winter—I'm sure I'd feel a lot more secure." Yet one more announces, "I've just bought five pounds of chestnut paste. Isn't it marvelous; and it makes me feel quite well off."

And what I would want would be many shelves of herbs and spices, and a haphazard herb garden with nothing correctly labeled, and a lizard guarding it from a rock, and a kitten in drunken wantonness in the catnip. Then I, too, might feel secure.

I would have basil, bay, and marjoram; oregano, parsley, and dill; and a rosemary branch from the ceiling. I would have chervil, sage, and tarragon; savory and saffron and thyme. There would be seeds: celery, sesame, cumin, and mustard; anise, caraway, cardamom, coriander, fennel, and dill; poppy and nutmeg. Then there would be pepper, whole and ground, and allspice and cinnamon and cloves. I would have cassia buds and mace. And the chili powder and paprika and curry powder would glow in the center of it all.

I would have a tiny German nutmeg grater and a porcelain mortar and pestle. And last, and very much, a tall jar full, full, full of vanilla beans.

Then, perhaps, I would be a secure, and very rich poet.

But the truly Poor Poet must forgo this shelf. When he craves a spicy dish or heady sauce, it is often far wiser to buy pre-packaged foods than to invest in a collection of spices when only a pinch of each will be used.

The basement walls that support my house are supported in turn by the usual motley—plus a case of beautiful, if empty, wine bottles, an outgrown dog harness, and three dozen ink cans that would be fine for storage, if only there were an easy way to remove the ink—in addition to a box that illustrates the point about spices.

Acquaintances who have lived nearby, only to move on, will say, as departure approaches, "I've nowhere to pack these spices, so here. Anyway, you cook a lot."

True, but the box today contains six full tins of cayenne. Enough for a lifetime of pear and cottage cheese salads with sufficient left over to keep the cat away from the favorite plant until one or the other dies of old age. In tins full to almost empty is nutmeg to make bread pudding twice a week for eleven years. Or, if combined with the jars of whole cloves and shakers of cinnamon, pomander balls for this not too small community.

There are further treasures in the box, their full use not yet tabulated. Note, too, that although an inveterate Easter-egg maker, I have inherited such a constant rainbow of food coloring that it has been unnecessary to purchase egg dyes at any time during the past nine years.

But if the Poor Poet intends to remain in one place for any period, or is willing to take his seasonings with him, he must start his collection with little tins of these herbs and spices that only he cannot do without. Such as basil and marjoram, and rosemary and thyme.

Sliced tomatoes in summer need olive oil and basil; stewed tomatoes in winter need basil; and omelets and scrambled eggs need it.

Soups need marjoram, as do eggs when the basil runs out. And meat loaves and stews and stuffings are just meat and vegetable and bread without it.

Rosemary in wine jelly and in all meats and poultry and good thick soups.

Thyme for tomatoes and fish and meat and poultry and stews.

For spices the Poor Poet must have paprika because it's pretty and pepper because it's necessary. He must have dried mustard so he can mix his own mustard sauce to taste. Or make a poultice.

He must have cinnamon for apples and for toast. And whole cloves to chew, and nutmeg for milk punch.

Then he will need chili powder and curry powder to remind him that life is love and warm and that the sun is hot. And flour and salt and oil and wine vinegar and a wire basket of garlic. And coffee and tea.

Too, the Poor Poet needs something to cook in and something to eat from. He needs two pots and lids. Or one double boiler, for this is really three pots. He needs a frying pan with a lid and non-burnable handle, so it can go into the oven. He needs a loaf pan and a cookie sheet and a big French knife; and a wooden spoon and a fork with a long handle. And a bowl and cup and plate and glass; a knife, a fork, and spoon for each person who is going to eat.

Such was the inventory of my first "kitchen".

For although there was at last steady employment, it would be six weeks until the first check arrived. And during those forty-two days I must eat—sitting down—and so make a kitchen in the far corner that contained a wash tub for sink and a two-burner hot plate for stove.

The double boiler, a good one, was a gift, and is still in constant use. I was early to discover that one could make Poor Poet's Soufflé in the top part while heating water for tea or instant coffee in the bottom.

The frying pan was a heavy, war-surplus model that tended to rust whenever the least bit of fog blew in from Point Loma. But it was good for stews, as well as the expected frying tasks. And it led to experimentation with ovenless cookies. Because it had a metal handle, it accompanied me (rust spots and all) through a series of apartments with ovens, or sometimes not-ovens, depending on the economic status of the moment.

The loaf pan and cookie sheet came somewhat later, for without an oven their utility is questionable. Although a loaf pan is a fine place to store silverware or bits of chalk and string. Or unpaid bills.

Purchase of the French knife was, at the time, a wildly extravagant gesture. The hand-me-down hunting knife and the pocket knife, a relic of Camp Fire Girl days, did not really have to be augmented. Just yet. But ownership of a French knife became an obsession then, and there is still pride and delight in using the same knife today. So that over the years I have become firmly convinced that—if one must limit himself to one knife—this is the one to own.

It came from the best cutlery shop in San Diego. Its 10-inch blade, made of high carbon cutlery steel (not the soon-to-lose-its-fine-edge stainless) was a mere point at the end, broadening out to two inches at the base, with the steel running right through the handle, which was firmly riveted in place. It weighed over half a pound. Its manipulation was easy, and the need for the design and weight readily apparent. The pointed end was held, as though hinged, against a cutting board, and the food to be sliced was pushed under the blade. For fine chopping, the point was steadied with one hand while the other powered the knife.

This knife, because of its weight and keen blade, was also good for slicing the infrequent roast, turkey, or ham. And—although I suppose its designers never intended it—for peeling assorted fruits and vegetables, slicing bread, or splitting whole chickens.

On occasional picnics, where hot dogs were cooked on skewers fashioned from wire coat hangers, it was used to chop kindling. And, on one darkly foggy night, to pilfer bamboo for fishing poles.

The first few bowls and plates were cheap Mexican pottery that was not at all durable but was decorated in lavish, spirit-lifting colors. The cups were seconds, the work of an uninspired potter at best, and the glasses were really assorted goblets, mustard steins, and jelly jars from Goodwill.

The flatware, if it could be called that, was the remains of a family picnic set, with plastic handles (a mistake) in red, green, and yellow.

Such was the collection that, when all was ready for dinner, it proved, if nothing else, that a Poor Poet could set a colorful table—as the many ladies' magazines advise.

But more important, perhaps, was that there was fresh bread and a dish of butter. A bottle of wine, and a candle for the table.

And so the nickel dinner grew. Sometimes wildly, so that its cost was almost a dollar, this crass expenditure precipitating an abrupt return to the nickel dinner in its original form. But, between these extremes, a recipe collection began to evolve. Shoe boxes, folders, drawers held the expanding medley. When moving time came, as it did so often for so long, empty spaces in the recipe "files" were stuffed with assorted socks, soap, stamps, or screws. Again, recipes were jotted on flyleaves of books, match folders, old letters.

More than one business house has received a check along with the notation for a stew or broth scrawled on the back of the bill. During a brief stint at advertising, it was one day discovered that the recipe for Russian Pancakes had been worked out on the margin of an otherwise pristine piece of copy.

Haphazard as all this was, and still is, even with the addition at last of a neat set of filing drawers—the recipes, except for an occasional gala dish, were Poor Poet variety. And, somehow (probably because they were referred to most often), those more closely approximating the nickel dinner were filed in the front.

So it became possible, in hard times, to reach for the first card in any section and come up with a nickel dinner. Or, in affluent periods, to select something extravagant by merely reaching to the back.

And, give or take a few pennies for seasonal price fluctuations, that is how this book has been set up.

The Nickel Dinner and How It Grew

For the first expansion of the nickel dinner (which today really comes closer to twenty-five cents, considering the butter and wine) the now not so Poor Poet might consider minestrone.

It must first have been made in the country, and over a charcoal fire, with herbs and pastes and the vegetables at hand. It breathes warmth and love and vegetable rows, which belie its humble ingredients.

MINESTRONE, PIEDMONT STYLE ❧ 4

    2 or 3 *small potatoes, diced*
    ¼ *head cabbage, shredded*
    1 *large zucchini, diced*
    1 or 2 *stalks celery, diced*
    1½ *cups raw vegetables at hand (peas, green beans,*
        carrots, etc., preferably fresh, not frozen)
    1 *one-pound can kidney beans*
    8 *cups water*
    2 *tablespoons each olive oil and butter*
    ½ *tablespoon dried basil leaves*
    3 *cloves garlic*
    ¼ *teaspoon salt*
    3 *tablespoons grated Parmesan cheese*

Bring the water to a boil in a large pot, dump in all the vegetables, cover and simmer for an hour. In the meantime mash together the oil, butter, basil, garlic, salt, and cheese. Just before serving, drop this paste into the soup and stir and simmer for about five minutes.

This, along with the basic nickel dinner, will serve four hungry poets, or one hungry poet and three friends.

It's to be eaten when the weather is cold and ominous and threatening. Should, however, the little check arrive on a summer day, a better choice might be a cold soup.

POOR POET'S BORSCH ℘ 4

The advantages of this soup are several-fold. It takes neither stirring nor watching over a steamy kettle, although its total effect is that it was brewed there. This, then, means that what is saved in fuel can go toward the foreseeable rainy or foggy or snowy day—paper, paint, or typewriter ribbon.

1 *one-pound can shoestring beets*
1 *10½-ounce can condensed bouillon*
2 *cups buttermilk*
3 *tablespoons brown sugar*
3 *tablespoons lemon juice*
½ *teaspoon salt*
⅛ *teaspoon pepper*
1 *tablespoon chopped onion*

Dump all the ingredients into a bowl or jar, stir well, cover, and chill thoroughly, preferably overnight.

STILL LIFE OMELET ℘ 4–6

This is for when the first check isn't quite so small, or when a still life is being dismantled or the refrigerator cleaned. It is an elastic recipe and the vegetables can be varied with almost anything that strikes the fancy— and good taste.

¼ teaspoon each thyme,
    basil, parsley, salt, and
    pepper
¼ cup milk
2 tablespoons olive oil
1 clove garlic, minced
2 onions, chopped
1 large tomato, cut in
    small chunks

2 stalks celery, sliced
1 green pepper, sliced,
    seeds removed
1 large zucchini, sliced
4 eggs
    dash of Tabasco sauce
    grated Parmesan cheese

Soak the herbs, salt and pepper in milk. Sauté garlic and onion in hot olive oil, then add the other vegetables and cook, covered, about 10 minutes, or until tender-crisp. Set aside to cool slightly. Beat eggs thoroughly with the herb-milk mixture and Tabasco. Pour over the vegetables and sprinkle with Parmesan. Place the omelet in a 350° oven until the eggs are just set.

Or, if there's no oven, do all the cooking on top of the stove. In this case, save the cheese to sprinkle over just before serving.

Don't forget the roll and butter. Or the wine.

CATS'LLEATIT

This was concocted when a bigger than expected check arrived. I was hungry for lots of meat, and the cats were, too. For, when I wandered through the kitchen to note the progress of my dinner, the cats had eaten a good share of it all up.

Cats'lleatit is manufactured from equal parts of heart, liver, tongue, kidney, sweetbreads, and/or brains (eater's choice) along with a handful each of diced salt pork and sliced onions. And a clove or two of garlic for those who like it.

Fry the salt pork. Cut the meats in small pieces and roll in flour. Brown well. Add the onion and garlic and a good shake of salt and pepper. Turn down the heat and add water to half cover the meat. Simmer, covered, for an hour, or until the meat is tender. Check the progress every so often, for the result should not be dry. Neither should it be awash. A bit of red wine, added now and then, adds to the flavor and doesn't seem to result in tipsy cats.

And, as the state of no funds at all is inevitably alleviated by the littlest check—or the biggest check ever —and back to the beginning and always, and over, and endlessly; so follow the Poor Poet's dinners.

For no matter how desperate the poet, his soul and stomach must, eventually (and preferably somewhat often), be pampered and spoiled and catered to with a really gala dinner. If only that later he can dream wistfully over his nickel dinner and through this paint or pot, or write or compose a little harder and a little better, and thus with greater and more tangible meaning and result.

For the truly gala dinner gives hope.

And the rules for hope are three: Always have something outrageously expensive. Serve it in the grandest manner. And—always use butter.

A Dinner for Instilling Hope

JELLIED CONSOMMÉ WITH CHOPPED NASTURTIUM LEAVES
CORNISH GAME HENS FLAMBÉES
WILD RICE MOLD
ASPARAGUS TIPS WITH MAÎTRE D'HÔTEL BUTTER
SALAD OF ENDIVE
CHARDONNAY
STRAWBERRIES ROMANOFF
COFFEE
TRIPLE SEC

$\frac{1}{2}$ *cup butter*
6 *Cornish game hens*
1 *pound mushrooms, sliced*
6 *shallots*
5 *ounces apricot brandy*
4 *tablespoons Marsala or sherry*
2 *egg yolks*
2 *cups heavy cream*
$\frac{1}{2}$ *teaspoon salt, pepper*
$\frac{1}{2}$ *pound wild rice, cooked and molded*

Rub the hens with salt and pepper and sauté in butter for 20 minutes, or until golden. Remove them from the pan and place in a hot oven to continue cooking. Toss the mushrooms and shallots in the butter and stir gently for about 5 minutes, or until the shallots are glassy. Reduce heat and add 1 ounce of brandy and the wine. Stir well to deglaze the pan. Beat egg yolks with the cream and add gradually, stirring until the sauce is well blended and thickened.

Arrange the hens on a platter around the molded rice. Dress with sprigs of parsley. Pour the remaining brandy over the hens and ignite. As the flame dies, drench them with the sauce and serve without delay.

SOUPS

The soup stone of Yeats' traveler may be the safest guide whenever the mood strikes for a pot of broth—thick or thin, hot or cold. Imagination and mystery and fancy make good soup. Renounceable here are the exact measurements and strict adherence to ingredients, paramount in the building of cakes or soufflés.

If the refrigerator affords space, a jar for collecting juices drained from vegetables, and a plastic bag for peels of carrots and potatoes (scrubbed), lettuce leaves, asparagus stems, and celery tops, is the beginning.

Tag ends of vegetables and meats can be incorporated, almost with abandon. Recalled is one superb dish whose base was French onion soup and potato salad. It has never been properly duplicated.

The remains of a bottle of white wine belong in vegetable soup or one with a poultry base. A dash of sherry goes into fish chowders, and red wine or a bit of strong coffee in soups with meat.

With boning knife and bravado, the Poor Poet can turn a pot roast of beef into steaks and soup bones; a chicken into the bases for Chicken Edgewood or Congee.

Or, if the boning knife is still being saved for, a handful of ground meat, simmered briefly and skimmed of fat, is not to be frowned upon. Nor is an appraisal of the butcher shop for lamb or chicken necks, a slice of beef heart, or even an official order of soup bones.

Insurance against want of all these, or the strength to shop, is a small store of bouillon cubes, vegetable and chicken stock bases.

Hot Soups for Cold Days

Winter reigns over the earth—a month for each of the pomegranate seeds with which Proserpina broke her fast. Often, during these months, poverty seems lurking at the heels of poets and others. It is, then, the time for hot soup in variety and abundance.

SANTAYANA'S GARLIC SOUP   ๕ 2

It was Santayana, I believe, who spoke of an excellent garlic soup his mother made. A descendant:

8 *large cloves garlic, sliced thin*
3 *or* 4 *slices French bread*
4 *tablespoons olive oil*
4 *cups water*
1 *beef bouillon cube*
4 *eggs*
½ *teaspoon salt and a little pepper*
1 *tablespoon grated Parmesan cheese*
1 *tablespoon minced parsley*

Heat half the olive oil in a saucepan and *slowly* cook the garlic until it becomes golden. Add the water and bouillon cube and simmer, covered, for 10 minutes or longer. In the meantime, fry the bread in the remaining oil and put into deep bowls, sprinkling the grated Parmesan on top. Now, poach the eggs in the soup. As soon as they are done place them on the bread slices, pour over the soup, and top with parsley.

This soup, along with a green salad, a crusty roll or two, a bit of cheese, and a bottle of red wine, is a big meal for two.

ADAM'S BREAD SOUP ᘓ 2

Adam studied theology in a little summerhouse under redwood and bay and madrone. The walls were solid with books in many languages. He said they afforded insulation—from without—as this soup does from within.

4 *cups bouillon or meat stock*
2 *frankfurters, cut in pieces*
2 *poached eggs*
2 *slices toast*
   salt and pepper

Heat the frankfurters in the bouillon. Make a little arrangement of toast and egg, salt and pepper in two bowls and pour the hot soup over all.

CONGEE ᘓ 4–6

Here's a good way to put to use chicken giblets, necks and backbones. Or substitute white fish or small shrimp. Congee is thick—almost a porridge. Chopped Chinese parsley, if available, is good sprinkled over. Or a little ground coriander. Sesame crackers go well on the side.

½ *pound chicken giblets*
6 *cups water*
¾ *cup raw rice*
4 *green onions, sliced*
1 *teaspoon chopped ginger root*
1 *teaspoon salt*
¼ *cup sherry*
1 *tablespoon soy sauce*
1 *large egg*

Cut giblets into small pieces. Combine all ingredients except the egg, cover and simmer 35 to 45 minutes, stirring occasionally and adding more water if necessary. When the rice has turned into a porridge, stir in a beaten egg. Serve immediately with additional soy sauce on the side.

GREEN PEA SOUP   ℧ 2–4

1 *cup fresh or frozen peas*
1 *cup water*
½ *cup evaporated milk*
1 *chicken bouillon cube*
½ *teaspoon salt*
1 *canned chili pepper*

Bring water to a boil. Toss in peas, salt, bouillon cube, and the pepper, seeded and sliced. Cover and simmer 10 to 15 minutes. Add milk and heat, but do not boil, and that's all there is to it. Except, of course, for those individuals who are carried away by the Christmas spirit, and so add a plop of sour cream and a dash of cayenne or paprika to each serving.

WATER CRESS SOUP   ℧ 4–6

What better reason to gather water cress on a spring day?

4 *cups water*
4 *chicken bouillon cubes*
¼ *cup shredded cooked pork or chicken*
¼ *cup finely sliced celery*
¼ *cup finely sliced water chestnuts or bamboo shoots (optional)*
2 *green onions, sliced*
1 *tablespoon soy sauce*
1 *cup chopped water cress, firmly packed*

Dissolve bouillon cubes in water and bring to boil. Add pork, celery, water chestnuts, onions, and soy. Cover and simmer 5 minutes. Increase heat, add the water cress, stir, and serve immediately.

TIN CAN CHOWDER ◖ 4–6

An impressive dish, this chowder is ready in a half hour . . . not counting the dash to the store, where French bread or pilot biscuits, red wine, and the makings for a green salad should also be procured.

4 *slices bacon*
1 *medium onion*
1 *10½-ounce can frozen potato soup or* 1 *package dehydrated type*
1 *can evaporated milk*
1 *bay leaf*
⅛ *teaspoon pepper*
1 *one-pound can salmon, shrimp, or lobster, or a combination*
½ *cup sherry*
salt to taste

Chop and sauté the bacon and onion. Add potato soup, milk, bay leaf, pepper, and fish. Cover and simmer 15 to 20 minutes. If the soup seems too thick, add a little water. Stir in sherry and salt just before serving.

SOUPAS ◖ 10–12

The Portuguese in California celebrate the Holy Ghost Festival in early summer. Following the parade and church service, guests (and everyone is a guest, for this is what the festival is about) line up at long tables made from planks and sawhorses for a feast of soupas, bread, salad, and new wine. Then there is dancing, and more eating, and so the day goes.

Once, unable to attend the local festival, I was presented with a gallon of soupas and the following recipe.

5 *pounds pot roast*
½ *of a 3-ounce can pickling spices*
   salt and pepper
¼ *teaspoon cumin seed powder*
8 *or* 10 *stalks celery*
4 *large onions*
3 *or* 4 *cloves garlic*

Put the meat in a large kettle and cover with water. Cut celery, onions, and garlic in generous pieces and add, along with pickling spices tied in a cheesecloth, salt, pepper, and cumin. Cover and simmer 2 or 3 hours until the meat falls from the bones, which are then removed. Taste for seasoning. A little vinegar may be added for extra tang. Serve in large bowls along with broken pilot crackers or pieces of French bread.

Cold Soups for Hot Days

Soups from scratch: the artisanship that requires a variety of vegetables, meats, and herbs—a French knife and big wooden spoon—a large pot. These are the soups to be preferred.

But not always.

Soups made mostly from opening tins find their places. Especially on hot days.

Like the foregoing, these cold soups invite experimentation. They may be of almost any (but not every) combination. And if the weather suddenly changes, most can be transferred to the stove and served steaming.

Soups from tins can be elegant, served up in mugs, tumblers, goblets, or small bowls that can be held in the hand.

But they must be the accompaniment of fresh bread and a big pat of butter.

MADRAS ASPARAGUS   ଓ 2–3

1 *can cream of asparagus soup*
1 *soup can milk*
½ *cup plain yogurt or 2 tablespoons dry white wine*
    dash of salt
    curry powder to taste

Combine and mix well the soup, milk, yogurt or wine, and salt. Chill for several hours. Top each serving with a small mound of curry powder.

CHICKEN AND SESAME   ଓ 3–4

1 *can condensed cream of chicken soup*
1 *soup can milk*
1 *teaspoon soy sauce*
1 *or 2 tablespoons sherry*
    toasted sesame seeds

Combine and mix well the first four ingredients. Chill for several hours and pour into small bowls. Sprinkle toasted sesame seeds over each serving. A few water cress leaves, a sprig of parsley, or a pair of short pine needles (the latter not to be eaten) make a good topper.

Toast sesame seeds in a heavy pan over medium heat. It's advisable to use a lid, so that the seeds don't fly over the kitchen in the toasting process.

CELERY BRACER

1 *can cream of celery soup*
1 *soup can milk*
2 *eggs*
   dash each of salt and Tabasco
   freshly grated nutmeg

Fill a quart jar about one-third with crushed ice. Add all ingredients but the nutmeg. Fasten down the lid and shake until contents are well iced and blended. Strain, or not, into two or three tall glasses. Grate a little nutmeg over each serving.

SUMMER DAY PEA SOUP

𝚌 4–6

1 *10½-ounce can condensed green pea soup*
2 *cups buttermilk*
   curry powder, toasted chopped almonds, or garlic
   croutons

Mix and chill well the soup and buttermilk. Serve topped with a little curry powder, almonds, or croutons.

CLIFF HANGER

𝚌 2

Purposely lacking in spirits, this brew is best on the rocks and immediately preceding the tackling of an heroic deed. Like changing a typewriter ribbon.

1 *can condensed beef broth or consommé*
1 *soup can tomato or vegetable juice*
   lemon wedges
1 *or 2 nasturtium leaves, chopped*

Fill two tall glasses with ice cubes and pour in the broth and tomato juice. Stir or not, depending on the penchant for a marbleized effect. Float the chopped nasturtium leaves and lemon wedges on top.

ICED BLACK BEAN CUP ⟡ 2–3

1 *can condensed black bean soup*
1 *soup can water*
1 *jigger sherry, or more (or 1 tablespoon Jamaica rum)*
lemon, sliced paper thin, or grated hard-cooked egg, or sour cream

Combine the soup, water, and sherry or rum. Beat well and allow to chill several hours. Serve in mugs or small bowls, with the lemon or grated egg on top, or a gob of sour cream.

Toasted rye crackers or water biscuits with anchovies, cherry tomatoes in a bowl of ice, and deviled eggs (in this case skip the grated egg on the soup) make a memorable lunch.

COLD CUCUMBER SOUP (DRINKABLE) ⟡ 4

2 *cups cucumbers, finely diced*
1 *cup chicken broth*
$\frac{1}{4}$ *cup green onions, minced*
1 *stalk parsley, minced*
2 *cups yogurt*
1 *teaspoon salt*
$\frac{1}{16}$ *teaspoon pepper*
dash Tabasco

This is easiest to make in an electric blender, but with patience and a good French knife, the vegetables can be well macerated. It should, in any case, be made a day ahead. The procedure is simply to get all the ingredients as well blended as possible and then to chill and chill.

COLD CUCUMBER SOUP (SPOONABLE)

3 *cups yogurt*
1 *cup water*
2 *cups finely diced cucumbers*
½ *cup currants*
½ *teaspoon dill weed*
2 *teaspoons minced mint leaves*
3 *tablespoons minced green onions*
1 *tablespoon minced parsley*
  salt and pepper

Beat the yogurt and water until smooth. Stir in the other ingredients and chill well, preferably overnight.

CHLODNIK

4 *cups Poor Poet's Borsch* (*page* 9)*
½ *cup chopped cooked shrimp, ham, or veal*
1 *cucumber, diced*
1 *green onion, sliced*
4 *or* 5 *radishes, sliced*
2 *or* 3 *hard-cooked eggs, chopped*
½ *cup beet greens or spinach, shredded* (*optional*)
1 *small dill pickle, sliced, or* 1 *teaspoon dill weed*
  salt and pepper

Mix all the ingredients, chill well, and serve in soup plates. The addition of some cottage cheese will stretch the portions to include one unexpected guest.

* If it's inconvenient to make the borsch, substitute 1 quart buttermilk and 1 cup diced or shoestring beets with juice.

SALADS

The professional-type gourmet spends a lifetime crunching through an infinity of iced lettuce dressed solely with olive oil, wine vinegar, salt, and cracked pepper.

The Poor Poet may, for a time, emulate such elegance. That is, until the day the produce market is blown away by a hurricane, or truck farm crops collapse under a late snow, or rabbits get into the vegetable garden behind the house. Then, rather than risk the threat of scurvy, the Poor Poet will devise something new in the line of salads, and very good, too.

Rabbits were the instigators for most of the following.

Not-Quite Salads

CUCUMBERS, ও 2–4
HANS CHRISTIAN ANDERSEN

2 *long cucumbers*	$\frac{1}{4}$ *cup water*
2 *teaspoons salt*	$\frac{1}{4}$ *cup vinegar*
2 *tablespoons dill weed*	$\frac{1}{4}$ *cup sugar*

Do not peel or seed the cucumbers, slice paper thin, sprinkle with salt and chill overnight. When ready to serve, drain cucumbers and mix with the remaining ingredients. Additional chilling blends the flavor nicely.

This dish can serve as salad, relish, sandwich filling, or edible decoration. Good, too, with sour cream.

VEGETABLES QUO VADIS   ℭ 4–6

¼ *cup olive oil*
1 *cup water*
2 *tablespoons wine vinegar*
½ *teaspoon salt*
4 *peppercorns*
2 *stalks parsley*
½ *teaspoon each chervil, tarragon, and thyme*
1 *bay leaf*
1 *clove garlic, mashed*
3 *or so cups of any or all of the following: sliced zuc-chini, mushrooms, diced eggplant, sliced onion, sliced carrots, asparagus stalks, celery hearts, cauliflower buds, green beans, sliced green or red peppers*

Combine all ingredients except the vegetables and bring to a boil. Add vegetables and simmer until they are barely tender. Remove vegetables and simmer the sauce until it is reduced by half. Strain it over the vegetables and chill well before serving.

This is good with, among other things, meat and cheese with crisp rolls, butter, and wine.

With determination, this salad can be kept several weeks.

4 *large zucchini*	1 *large clove garlic*
flour	1 *can anchovies*
salt and pepper	*juice of 2 lemons*
¾ *cup olive oil*	1 *bunch parsley*

Cut unpeeled zucchini into ½-inch-thick rounds. Dredge them in flour, salt, and pepper and fry quickly in ½ cup hot olive oil. They should be crisp and gold on the outside and still uncooked in the center. Drain on paper towels. Mash the other ingredients well with the remaining olive oil—more if necessary. Fill a dish with alternate layers of zucchini and anchovy-parsley sauce. Cover and chill at least 24 hours before serving.

SALSA   ℘ 6–8

For years I thought this was a salad called Salsa, only to be informed recently that it's a soup called Gazpacho. But habit being what it is, it will always remain Salsa— and a salad.

½ *loaf white bread*	2 *hard-cooked eggs,*
4 *cups canned or fresh*	*chopped*
tomatoes	½ *teaspoon salt*
1 *clove garlic, mashed*	¼ *teaspoon pepper*
1 *onion, chopped*	1½ *teaspoons Worcester-*
4 *stalks celery, chopped*	*shire*
1 *green pepper, chopped,*	*dash Tabasco*
seeds removed	8 *tablespoons olive oil*
1 *small cucumber, chopped*	4 *tablespoons wine vinegar*
1 *can green chillies, chopped*	*or lemon juice*

Soak bread in water, drain and mash with the tomatoes. Dump in all other ingredients, stir nicely, and let chill for a minimum of 4 hours. Stir well again before serving. The absent-minded poet, who forgets to add the celery, green pepper, onion, and chilies, will come up with an excellent, though less fiery Salsa.

CELERY VICTOR   ℞ 8

2 *large bunches celery*
1 *quart chicken broth*
¾ *cup salad oil*
⅓ *cup dry white wine*
1 *tablespoon lemon juice*
1 *teaspoon salt*

¼ *teaspoon cracked black*
  pepper
1 *teaspoon grated onion*
  dash each Tabasco,
  Worcestershire sauce,
  and paprika
16 *anchovy fillets*

Trim celery to make bunches about 6 inches long, and then quarter each bunch lengthwise. Bring chicken broth to boil, add celery, and cook for about 20 minutes, or until barely tender. Remove the pan from the heat and allow the celery to cool in the broth. Now drain the celery and lay in a shallow dish. Combine all remaining ingredients except anchovies; pour over celery hearts. Chill for several hours or overnight. To serve, lay a celery heart on each plate, accompanied by a leaf or 2 of crisp lettuce. Criss-cross 2 anchovy fillets over each heart, and drizzle with a little of the dressing in which the celery was marinated.

Hungry Poet Salads

When the weather's too hot, or the fuel bill has been too high, or there isn't a stove at all, it's good to have big, full-meal salads. More dignified than eating something from a can and less extravagant than picking up bits and pieces from the delicatessen.

In any case, the crisp roll and butter, and wine add infinite pleasure.

ARTISTS' SPECIAL   ℧ 2–4

1 *pint cottage cheese*
¼ *cup mayonnaise*
2 *tablespoons prepared horse-radish*
3 *green onions, chopped*
   salt and pepper
   lettuce, broken fairly small

Toss everything but the lettuce gently and patiently with a fork, and then plop on 3 or 4 plates well-piled with lettuce. If there's not enough lettuce, use some chopped raw spinach. And if there's neither lettuce nor spinach, eat as is.

TIVOLI GARDEN BEANS   ℧ 6

2 *ounces Italian salami, shredded*
1 *one-pound can green beans*
½ *teaspoon garlic salt*
¼ *teaspoon dry mustard*
2 *tablespoons olive oil*
1½ *tablespoons tarragon vinegar*
½ *cup diced celery*
¼ *cup sliced radishes*
2 *green onions, sliced*
1 *or 2 hard-cooked eggs, sliced*

Drain the beans, and mix with all but the last four items. Cover and chill overnight. Just before serving toss in the celery, radishes, onions and eggs and mix once again.

CABBAGE AND PEANUTS

    2 cups shredded cabbage
    1 firm pear, cored and diced
    3 tablespoons chopped salted peanuts
    1 tablespoon cider vinegar
    ½ teaspoon celery salt
    6 tablespoons sour cream

Toss all ingredients and chill before serving. This is also good hot, served with mashed potatoes. In this case, steam the cabbage until it is just wilted and then toss with other ingredients.

PILAF SALAD

    leftover pilaf (page 58) or rice
    olive oil
    tarragon vinegar
    chopped celery
    pitted black and/or green olives
    chopped tomato
    red and green peppers, sliced, seeds removed
    salt, pepper, nutmeg, basil

The number of servings will depend on the amount of left-over pilaf or rice. In any case, the salad should be made while the pilaf is still warm, then allowed to chill overnight. Merely mix in all ingredients to taste, pile into a dish to be served the next day, or into a container to carry to a picnic.

PICNIC SALAD

1 head lettuce, broken   *1 or 2 lemons*
1 tin anchovy fillets   *salt, pepper, and garlic*
1 or 2 hard-cooked eggs

This is ideally suited for a picnic, for all ingredients are carried separately and mixing is done on the spot as follows: open anchovy tin and cut the fillets into short pieces, being careful not to lose any oil. Peel the eggs and cut them into the lettuce. Now dump in the tin of anchovies and their oil; salt, pepper, and garlic to taste; and squeeze over the juice of the lemons. Combine well and serve along with hunks of French bread and plenty of dry red wine.

VINTNERS' POTATO SALAD ℘ 8

In the hills of Berkeley is an old redwood house with a shower stall made from a telephone booth—intact except for the phone itself. On Telegraph Hill across the Bay is one made from a large wine vat. And this recipe for the owner's special potato salad.

$2\frac{1}{2}$ *pounds potatoes*
1 *cup dry white wine*
4 *hard-cooked eggs,*
  chopped
2 *stalks celery, chopped*
1 *onion, chopped*
2 *tablespoons capers*
2 *tablespoons chopped*
  parsley

1 *tablespoon celery seed*
1 *tablespoon seasoning salt*
$\frac{1}{2}$ *teaspoon pepper*
4 *tablespoons French*
  dressing
$\frac{1}{4}$ *cup each mayonnaise*
  and sour cream

Boil or bake the potatoes until tender, peel them, and slice into a bowl. Pour the wine over the hot potatoes and let sit for about an hour. In the meantime, mix together all other ingredients and, hoping the potatoes are still somewhat warm, fold the sauce into them. The result should not be mashed potato salad. Chill well for several hours before serving.

The potato salad addict might like a change now and then, and so substitute dill weed and a little chopped pickle or olives for the capers; or use caraway instead of celery seed.

This is the entire meal, except for the inevitable rolls, butter, and wine. And fruit and coffee later.

¼ *cup sour cream*
½ *teaspoon salt*
¼ *teaspoon pepper*
2 *tablespoons vinegar*
2 *cups diced cooked potatoes*
1 *hard-cooked egg, diced*
1 *cup cottage cheese*
3 *tablespoons minced onion*
½ *cup sliced celery*
1 *12-ounce tin luncheon meat, cut in strips*
    lettuce, carrot strips, radishes

Combine sour cream, salt, pepper, and vinegar and set aside. Toss potatoes, egg, cottage cheese, onion, celery, and luncheon meat into a large bowl. Add the sour cream mixture and stir lightly. Chill. Serve surrounded by lettuce, carrot strips, and radishes.

VEGETABLES IN SANDALS

This is pleasant to eat while wearing sandals and sitting in the sun. Good music, red wine, crisp rolls and butter complete this pastorale.

small tomatoes, quartered
boiled potatoes, sliced
green beans, cooked tender-crisp
several slices red onion, separated into rings
green pepper slices
cauliflower buds, cooked tender-crisp

pitted black olives
anchovy fillets
small can tuna
1 or 2 hard-cooked eggs, quartered
dressing of red wine vinegar, olive oil, Dijon mustard, salt, and pepper

Chill the vegetables, fish, and eggs and just before serving toss with the dressing. The whole is elegant served on a foundation of French bread slices or pilot biscuits.

Three Necessary Dressings

These are for *green* salads (iceberg lettuce, romaine, spinach, water cress, and the like) and are as necessary to the salad tosser as a tube of white lead and a can of turpentine are to the painter.

Three rules for really good green salads: Have the greens and the salad bowl terribly cold. If not using a prepared-in-advance dressing, be sure to add oil first and vinegar the very last. Never, never combine the greens and dressing until the very moment of eating.

STUDIO SPECIAL

This is for last-minute tossing and will take care of two quarts or so of greens.

1 *clove garlic*
½ *cup olive oil*
1 *one-minute egg*
   several shakes paprika
   large shake salt
   freshly ground pepper
¼ *cup grated Parmesan*
   cheese
½ *teaspoon Worcestershire*
   juice of 1 *lemon*
¼ *cup red wine vinegar*
1 *cup croutons*

Rub a large bowl with garlic and dump in the vegetables. Sprinkle oil, paprika, salt, pepper, cheese, and Worcestershire over the lettuce. Plop in the egg. Toss thoroughly but lightly until each leaf is coated. Add the lemon, vinegar, and croutons and give a final toss. Serve immediately.

BLUE CHEESE DRESSING

This keeps well in the refrigerator. It's good to make when a long-forgotten and somewhat strong hunk of blue cheese finally comes to light in the far reaches of the cooler.

  ½ *cup crumbled blue cheese*
  ½ *cup salad oil*
  ¼ *plus cup wine vinegar*
     salt and pepper to taste
     dash of cayenne

Mash cheese and oil with a fork. Add the vinegar, a little at a time, and season to taste.

SOUR CREAM DRESSING

  ½ *pint sour cream or equal parts yogurt and sour*
     cream
  1 *tablespoon vinegar*
  1 *teaspoon sugar*
  ½ *teaspoon salt*
  ½ *teaspoon dry mustard*
  ½ *teaspoon celery seed*
     pepper to taste

Mix all the ingredients thoroughly. Let stand for a half hour or so to blend the flavors.

BUILDING WITH
EGGS AND CHEESE

No hen will lay her eggs for you
Unless they're placed in baskets, too.
—HAROLD LEWIS

Eggs, one of the most useful of the food products, are of infinite value to the Poor Poet. Not only are they necessary in a number of dishes as binder, clarifier, stabilizer, leavener, and garnish; but they may be served up almost as is for any meal during the day. Or night. And they look nice in a straw basket.

And, for the nutritionally minded, they are one of the few complete foods.

Not counting the Chinese method of preparing thousand-year eggs (which now, thanks to a new process, can be made "instantly") there are about a dozen approved egg cookery methods. But, for the Poor Poet, we stick primarily to scrambling or omelet methods—for their economic virtues alone.

Ways with Eggs

BAREFOOT OMELET   ℭ 4

If a cup or two of cold cooked spaghetti or noodles is substituted for the potatoes, this becomes Shoestring Omelet. So named in honor of the local poets who were recently apprised of the fact that it is against the law to run around in bare feet.

2 tablespoons butter or olive oil
2 boiled potatoes, sliced
4 eggs
2 tablespoons milk
1 tablespoon grated dry cheese
　salt and pepper

Brown the potatoes in butter. Beat eggs with milk, cheese, salt and pepper, and pour over the potatoes. Cook slowly, about 5 minutes on each side, or—if the flipping-over process is impracticable, proceed as for scrambled eggs.

Those who wish to spend the next several hours alone may add garlic to taste.

SCRAMBLED MATZOTHS ～ 4

6 matzoths soaked in water　　*salt and pepper to taste*
4 eggs, well beaten　　*butter*

Squeeze excess water from the matzoths (other crackers will do) and mix well with the eggs, salt, and pepper. Fry slowly in plenty of butter.

HYPNOTIC EYES

Although its creator claims this composition was designed primarily for laughs, it's good for a crowd or for buffet service. For each person:

2 slices bread　　*2 eggs*
1 tablespoon butter　　*1 tablespoon grated cheese*
4 tablespoons cream　　*salt, pepper, and paprika*

Remove the centers of the bread (use them later for Down and Out Eggs or for Bread Pudding) and brown the part that's left in butter. Sprinkle a baking dish with a little cream, lay in the bread rounds, and break a raw egg in the center of each slice. Sprinkle on the cheese and seasonings and a bit more cream. Bake in a moderate (350°) oven about 15 minutes, or until the eggs are set.

STEAMED EGGS ℧ 3–4

Handy for when there's only enough butter for the fresh rolls.

6 *eggs*   1 *tablespoon sherry*
1 *tablespoon soy sauce*   1 *3½-ounce can mushrooms*

Beat the eggs with the soy and sherry. Pour into the top of a double boiler that has been wiped with a little oil. Cover and steam until the eggs are almost set. Stir in the mushrooms and continue cooking until done.

DOWN AND OUT EGGS ℧ 4–6

A *big* breakfast as well as a boon to the one hot plate cooking setup.

¼ *pound bacon, diced (or leftover ham, luncheon meat,*
   bologna)
4 *eggs*
12 *crackers, crushed*
¼ *cup milk or water*
2 *tablespoons chopped onion*
   salt and pepper
6 *slices bread*
   grated cheese (optional)

Fry bacon until it is crisp. Meanwhile make a thin batter of the eggs, crackers, milk, salt, and pepper. Without draining the fat from the pan, sprinkle in the onions, cover the bottom of the pan with bread, and pour over the egg mixture. Cook for about 10 minutes over low heat; flip the whole thing over and continue cooking until the eggs are set. Sprinkle the grated cheese over just after the flipping.

HUEVOS RANCHEROS

This is an eye-opener from Ensenada where we once befriended a poet awaiting a long overdue fruit boat and points south. In the evenings we had tequila and limes for a dime, and in the mornings platters of huevos rancheros and big glasses of orange juice. For each serving:

3 *tortillas*
2 *eggs*
½ *cup enchilada sauce*
  Mexican hot sauce or Tabasco

Heat the tortillas in the top of a double boiler, or fry lightly, and place on a plate. Fry the eggs and slip them on top of the tortillas. Drown each serving in steaming hot enchilada sauce. Extra hot sauce is for the braver fire eaters.

SCRAMBLED EGGS WITH   ℭ 4
CURRY AND BLACK BUTTER

6 *eggs, well beaten*
1 *teaspoon curry powder*
¼ *teaspoon salt*
6 *tablespoons cream*
4 *slices bacon, diced*
1 *small onion, chopped fine*
½ *green pepper, chopped fine, seeds removed*
¼ *cup butter*

Dissolve the curry powder and salt in the cream and add to beaten eggs. Fry bacon until crisp, then sauté onion and pepper. Discard any excess fat and pour egg mixture into pan. Scramble slowly. Meanwhile, brown the butter in a saucepan and pour a little over each serving of eggs.

EGGS WITH BLACK BEANS   ⌘ 6

2 *tablespoons salad oil*	½ *soup can water*
1 *clove garlic, minced*	2 *tablespoons butter*
1 *large onion, chopped fine*	6 *eggs*
¾ *cup stewed tomatoes*	½ *cup grated cheese*
1 *can condensed black bean*	*salt and pepper*
soup	

Sauté the garlic and onion in oil until vegetables are light brown. Add the tomatoes, bean soup, and water; mix well and simmer for 10 minutes or so. Butter a large flat baking dish and break the eggs into it. Sprinkle them with salt, pepper, and cheese and spread the bean mixture on top. Dot with more butter and bake in a 375° oven until the eggs are set.

Serve with hot crisp rolls or steamed tortillas and butter.

Omelets

After Easter is a good time for omelets, the pre-holiday weeks having involved daily scrambled eggs so that enough shells can be blown clean for decorating and giving away. So far no acceptable method has been devised for blowing eggs and coming out with yolks and whites neatly separated.

Like Caruso this omelet did not really survive the San Francisco earthquake. Devised some years later, it takes its name from the fact, however, that had it been in the quake, it would no doubt have come through its puffy, light self. Unless a brick toppled on it.

4 *eggs, separated*
2 *tablespoons water*
2 *tablespoons flour*
½ *teaspoon salt*
⅛ *teaspoon pepper*
1 *tablespoon butter*

Eggs should be at room temperature to insure a successful omelet. Beat the whites and salt until stiff. Combine and beat the other ingredients (except butter) and fold most gently into the egg whites. Melt the butter in a big iron skillet over a low fire and pour in the batter. Cover the skillet and let cook for about 12 minutes. Now uncover the pan and put it into a slow oven to set the top. Slide the omelet out onto a warm plate, fill it with anything that seems reasonable and serve to four.

Reasonable fillings run from the usual creamed vegetables and meats to cottage cheese, chili beans, canned spaghetti, undiluted gumbo soup, or fried potatoes with lots of onions and a wash of cream.

LITTLE MASTERS' OMELET   ℭ 4

From the Baroque painters of Amsterdam, Haarlem, and Delft, this is for eating when funds are more readily available—and, anyway, tomorrow seems like a good day to make macaroons or meringues.

Whip up an '06 Omelet, but add a tablespoon chopped parsley and a pinch of fennel for seasoning. Then fill with the following:

1 *tablespoon butter*	½ *pint sour cream*
1 *tablespoon flour*	2 *egg yolks*
½ *cup rich milk*	*salt and pepper*

Prepare a white sauce with the butter, flour, and milk. Stir in the sour cream and then the egg yolks and seasonings. Keep stirring over a low flame until the filling is thickened.

THE SPOILED LOVER   ℃ 4

Well, why not? This calls for a dimly lighted room and grandmother's chafing dish—or some agile foot-work between stove and table.

Prepare the standby '06 Omelet, this time flavoring it with ¼ cup powdered sugar and ½ teaspoon vanilla. In a separate pan heat a jar of preserved mixed fruits, the juice thickened with a big spoonful of apricot jam and a little cornstarch. In yet another pan heat ½ cup rum or brandy.

When ready for the finale, slip the omelet onto a large plate, pile the fruit around, sprinkle with a little sugar, pour the warm rum over the fruit, and ignite. When the flame begins to flicker the omelet is ready to serve.

Dishes Incorporating Both Eggs and Cheese

POOR POET'S SOUFFLÉ I   ℃ 6

Although not a soufflé in the true sense of the word, this (and Soufflé II) is less traumatic for the nervous cook than is the genuine thing. Besides, it will turn out, in almost the worst of ovens.

12 *slices stale bread*
   butter
2 *cups cottage cheese*
1 *teaspoon horse-radish*
4 *eggs·*
2½ *cups milk*
½ *teaspoon salt and some pepper*

Butter both the bread slices and a baking dish large enough to hold 6 slices laid flat. Stir horse-radish into the cottage cheese and spread over the slices. Top with other slices, buttered on both sides, if possible. Beat remaining ingredients and pour over the bread. Let stand about 30 minutes. Bake for 30 to 40 minutes at 350°.

Last night's garlic bread makes a terrific soufflé. In this case, cut down on or completely omit the horse-radish, using instead additional crushed garlic.

POOR POET'S SOUFFLÉ II ꙮ 6

12 *slices stale bread*
½ *pound sharp cheese, sliced or grated*
2 *large onions*
6 *eggs*
2 *cups milk*
½ *teaspoon each salt and dry mustard and some*
   pepper

Build 2 layers of bread, cheese, and sautéed onions in a buttered baking dish. Beat the eggs, milk, and seasonings and pour over the bread. Let stand for an hour, then bake in a 300° oven for 45 minutes.

Rye bread with Swiss cheese is interesting. So is the addition of bacon, ham, or chipped beef. Caraway or poppy seeds add variety. And ¼ cup sherry in place of an equal quantity of milk is hardly to be frowned upon.

PRAGMATIC PIZZA

Here, the quantity of ingredients is dependent upon the appetites of the eaters.

French bread, sliced
garlic
olive oil
cottage cheese
paprika

Generously anoint French bread slices with garlic, then lay each slice in a baking pan covered with olive oil to about $\frac{1}{8}$ inch. Spread cottage cheese over the bread and sprinkle on a bit of paprika. Bake in a 375° oven until the cheese is bubbly, and prepare to eat immediately. A big green salad, perhaps with anchovies, and lots of red wine round out the menu.

AN ONION PIE   ひ 4

$1\frac{1}{2}$ *cups dry bread crumbs*
$\frac{1}{4}$ *teaspoon curry powder*
$\frac{1}{4}$ *teaspoon salt*
6 *tablespoons melted butter*
$1\frac{1}{2}$ *cups sliced or chopped*
    onion
2 *tablespoons butter*
$1\frac{1}{4}$ *cups milk*

1 *teaspoon salt*
$\frac{1}{4}$ *teaspoon paprika*
$\frac{1}{2}$ *teaspoon curry powder*
    dash of cayenne
$1\frac{1}{2}$ *cups sharp cheese,*
    grated
2 *eggs, beaten*

Combine the first 4 ingredients and line a deep pie pan, reserving $\frac{1}{4}$ cup crumb mixture. Sauté the onions in butter, add milk, and when it is hot, stir in the remaining seasonings and cheese. Allow to cool a bit before adding the eggs. Pour the filling into the crust and sprinkle remaining crumbs on top. Bake for 35 to 40 minutes, or until set, at 325°.

With a little mosaic work it's also possible to fashion a respectable crust from slices of several-day-old bread.

CHEESE PIE, LEFT BANK   ♋ 4–6

1 9-*inch unbaked pastry shell*
2 *cups cottage cheese*
2/3 *cup sour cream*
2 *cups mashed potatoes*
2 *eggs, well beaten*
1 *teaspoon salt*
3 *tablespoons onion, chopped*
3 *tablespoons pimiento or pimiento-stuffed green*
   olives, chopped
1½ *tablespoons butter*

Blend cottage cheese with sour cream. Beat in the potatoes and then all other ingredients except the butter. Use this to dot the top of the filling after it is poured into the pastry shell. Bake at 350° for 1 to 1¼ hours, or until filling is set.

Although this cheese pie is better hot, it is quite good cold, and so an excellent main dish for a picnic.

LAZY PIEROGI   ♋ 4–6

A big platter of Pierogi is superb, especially on a cool night. But the cottage cheese must be well drained or the dish is guaranteed to fall apart at least twice: once while being rolled on the floured board and again while cooking.

4 *eggs, separated*   1 *teaspoon sugar*
1 *tablespoon melted butter*   ½ *cup flour*
1 *pound dry cottage cheese*   ¾ *cup bread crumbs*
¼ *teaspoon salt*   4 *or so tablespoons butter*

Beat the cheese with the egg yolks and melted butter. Beat egg whites until quite stiff, then fold into the cheese mixture alternately with the flour, salt, and sugar. Roll the Pierogi on a floured board into 2-inch balls. Cook for 10 to 15 minutes in gently boiling water. Remove with a slotted spoon to a large platter and drizzle over crumbs that have been browned in butter.

TOPFENKNÖDEL ❧ 4

This cheese dumpling from Czechoslovakia may be served either as a main dish or as a dessert, or even a breakfast dish.

1 *pound dry cottage cheese*
2 *slices bread, soaked in water and drained*
2 *egg yolks*
1 *tablespoon flour*
2 *tablespoons bread crumbs*
½ *teaspoon salt*

Mix all ingredients well and set in refrigerator for an hour. Shape the dough into dumplings and dust with flour. Drop the dumplings into boiling salted water or stock, and boil gently for 5 to 10 minutes. Remove with a slotted spoon. Serve sprinkled with sugar and cinnamon and hot melted butter poured over all. Or serve as a soup along with the stock in which they were cooked.

RUSSIAN PANCAKES ❧ 4

Easier than blintzes, and almost as good.

1½ *pounds cottage cheese*
2 *egg yolks*
1 *whole egg*
½ *cup flour*
  butter
1 *quart, at least, sour cream*

Drain cottage cheese in a cheesecloth-lined sieve or colander. This takes overnight. Now, working with a large bowl, not the colander, beat in the yolks and whole egg and blend in the flour. Chill well, form into cakes no more than $\frac{1}{2}$ inch thick, roll in flour or fine crumbs, and fry until golden-brown in lots of butter. Serve topped with mounds of sour cream.

FONDUE FIRE ESCAPE   ও 4–6

Cooking on the fire escape is outlawed in most cities, but fun. However, this fondue will be just as successful if the chafing dish or hibachi is brought inside. And for honest-to-goodness informal dining: a double boiler on the stove, with everyone standing around.

In any case, make the fondue in the top part of a double boiler or in an earthenware casserole set in a pan of hot water.

> 1 *large clove garlic*
> $\frac{1}{2}$ *bottle dry white wine*
> 1 *pound Swiss cheese, grated*
> 3 *ounces Parmesan cheese, grated*
> 2 *tablespoons brandy*
>   *pinch of nutmeg*
>   *tray of bread, ham chunks, and parboiled vegetables*
>   *suitable for dipping*

Rub the casserole with cut garlic. Heat wine and add the cheese, stirring constantly until it is well melted and blended. When ready to serve, grate some nutmeg over the top and stir in the brandy.

Eaters then spear pieces of bread (or ham or vegetable) with forks and dip into the fondue.

A bottle of brandy or white wine should be kept at hand in case the fondue thickens too much. In any case, especially on the fire escape, the wine should not be drunk along with the fondue. Rather, strong coffee should follow.

FRIED CREAM CHEESE   ♋ 4–6

Here is a sophisticated version of the Monterey fishermen's delight. Their method is simply to take squares of very soft Jack or Tillamook cheese, roll it in crumbs, and fry in hot olive oil in which many cloves of garlic are bubbling. The cheese is eaten along with French bread, cold vegetables or a green salad, and wine.

> 2 *eggs*
> 3 *egg yolks*
> 1 *cup plus 2 tablespoons flour*
> ¼ *teaspoon salt*
>   *pepper and a little nutmeg*
> 1 *cup grated Swiss cheese*
> 1 *quart milk*
>   *fine bread or cracker crumbs*
>   *oil for frying*

Warm the milk. In the meantime, beat the eggs in the top of a double boiler. (Remember—lightly beaten eggs thicken better.) Alternately blend in the flour and milk. Stir in the salt, pepper, and nutmeg. Place the mixture over gently boiling water and allow to thicken while stirring constantly. Indispensable here: a wire whisk and patience. In about 10 minutes, when the mixture is the consistency of a thick white sauce, remove it from the heat, stir in the cheese, and turn it into a well-buttered pan. Cover and chill well.

When serving time comes, cut the cheese into inch-thick slices, dip in crumbs (dipping first into slightly beaten egg white makes a lighter crust), and fry quickly in hot oil. Garlic lovers are urged to toss several cloves of that bulb into the oil.

BEANS, PEAS, RICE, AND ASSORTED CEREALS

Venus gave Psyche three tasks to prove that she was deserving of Cupid's love. First, she was to separate into individual heaps an enormous storehouse of seeds of all kinds—wheat, beans, lentils, poppy, barley, and many others.

Although cereals are no longer piled in such slipshod fashion and, moreover, can rarely be bought in bulk from big sacks and boxes heaped along the wall, it is still best to sort through for an odd weed seed or pebble should one deserve love. A well-cooked and seasoned pebble under a new inlay can dampen romance.

For the non-bean-sorter, the person who doesn't like to cook from scratch—or doesn't have the time, or the money for fuel—there are more ready to eat concoctions on the market than there were kinds of seeds in Psyche's task. Some are quite good, but usually expensive. But any of them can be improved with tampering.

Catsup, mustard, molasses, cut-up ham, frankfurters or bacon, and a dash of strong black coffee, red wine, or rum are standbys.

Bean Dishes from Canned Beans

FIREBAUGH BEANS   ॐ 2

Firebaugh was a dusty farm labor town in the San Joaquin Valley when a young and unsuccessful writer lived primarily on this dish—which is good.

1 *one-pound can pork and*   1 *large tomato, chopped*
  beans (remove pork)   *salt and pepper*
1 *medium onion, chopped*

That's all. Mix it and eat it, although chilling for a few hours does improve the flavor.

CONDÉ   ॐ 2–4

$\frac{1}{4}$ *pound bacon, diced*   1 *#2$\frac{1}{2}$ can kidney beans*
4 *green onions, chopped* $\frac{1}{2}$ *cup evaporated milk*
2 *bay leaves*   1 *cup hot water*
  salt and pepper $\frac{1}{4}$ *teaspoon gumbo filé*
                      powder

Brown bacon and onion and add all ingredients except the filé powder. Cook over low heat for 15 minutes. Stir in filé powder and serve in bowls with crisp rolls and butter and a big green salad.

GRANT AVENUE BEANS   ॐ 6

This can be all mixed together and either heated well for winter eating or chilled for summer. Or eat it cold any time and save on the fuel bill.

2 *one-pound cans kidney beans, drained*
1 *clove garlic, crushed*
3 *tablespoons olive oil*
$\frac{1}{2}$ *cup red wine*
2 *tablespoons minced parsley*
$\frac{1}{2}$ *cup chopped olives*
  salt and pepper

ARTISTS' BAKED BEANS   ℃ 2

Another hot-or-cold concoction for two hungry artists.

1 *one-pound can baked beans*
1 *teaspoon prepared mustard*
2 *tablespoons chili sauce*
1 *cup cottage cheese*
½ *cup chopped onions*
1 *tablespoon minced parsley*

Mix together the first 3 ingredients and heat well.
Dump into a deep dish and top with the cottage cheese,
onion, and parsley, in that order. For hot weather eating,
skip fussing over the stove by mixing and chilling all
ingredients.

COUNTRY MOUSE BEANS   ℃ 4

"Better beans and bacon in peace than cakes and ale
in fear," says Aesop's Country Mouse to his cousin.
This is good for feeding visiting city mice, among others.

1 *large onion, chopped*
  butter
½ *cup green peppers, chopped, seeds removed*
½ *cup diced ham*
1 *can Italian tomato paste*
1 *cup red wine*
2 *#2 cans baked kidney beans*
8 *strips bacon*

Sauté the onion, pepper, and ham in a little butter.
Add the tomato paste and wine and cook and stir about
5 minutes. Dump in the beans and stir briefly before
turning the mixture into a casserole. Lay the bacon over
the top and bake for 30 minutes at 350°. This, along with
hard rolls, green salad, and the rest of the wine, will
please four city mice, with some left over for the cook.

BEANS AND SAUSAGE
FOR A COLD NIGHT

1 *pound sausage*
3 *cups cooked beans* (*any kind*)
1 *can tomato soup*
1 *teaspoon chili powder*
1 *small onion, chopped*
  salt and pepper

Brown the sausage and pour off the fat. Toss in the onions, and cook until they're limp. Now combine everything in a casserole and bake for about 40 minutes at 350°. Nice when the rain is beating on a roof that may or may not be leaking.

A BEAN DISH TO BE WARMED OVER ও 8

Bad luck to misplace this dish in the far reaches of the refrigerator. For such action would make the cook a wrongdoer, and thus punishable by the speaking beans of folklore, who exist solely to mete out punishments.

1 *pound ground beef*
1 *large onion, chopped*
1 *green pepper, chopped, seeds removed*
1 *can tomato-mushroom sauce*

1 *one-pound can tomatoes*
1 *6-ounce can mushroom stems and pieces*
2 *one-pound cans kidney beans*
  salt and pepper

Brown the meat in a little oil, adding the onion and green pepper when the meat is about half done. Drain off excess fat. Pour in the tomato-mushroom sauce and canned tomatoes, and stir both to mix and to break up the tomatoes. Simmer, with lid on, about 30 minutes, when it's time to add the mushrooms, beans, salt and pepper. Reheat the dish and eat, or hide it away for tomorrow.

1 *onion, chopped*
1 *tablespoon bacon fat*
2 *one-pound cans pink beans*
½ *teaspoon dry mustard*
1 *can chicken gumbo soup*
1½ *cups canned tomatoes*
6 *frankfurters, sliced*

Brown the onion in the fat. Drain the beans (save the liquid) and add, along with all the other ingredients. Stir to mix, cover the pot, and let simmer gently for a half hour or so. Stir every so often and add a little bean liquor if the mixture seems dry. Serve with rice and brown bread.

WESTERN CHILI   ∾ 8–12

Joseph P. MacCarthy noted that, to be happy in New England, one must make sure in advance that his obituary appears in the *Boston Transcript*—and, eat beans on Saturday night.

The western version of a Boston Saturday night is chili. It's eaten in the kitchen in winter and in the patio in summer. Great kettles of it are lugged to the mountains or the desert or the shore. Or to an ailing friend whose digestive tract is still in order.

1 *pound ground beef*
1 *large onion, chopped*
1 *clove garlic, mashed*
1 *green pepper, chopped, seeds removed*
2 *one-pound cans red beans*
1 *#2½ can tomatoes*
1 *cup tomato juice*

2 *bouillon cubes*
½ *teaspoon each basil, oregano, cumin, and thyme*
1 *tablespoon chili powder, or more to taste*
1 *cup chopped ripe olives salt to taste*

Brown the beef in a little oil, adding the onion, garlic, and pepper when the meat is about half done. Dump everything into a large kettle and simmer, covered, at least an hour. If the chili is made ahead and reheated, it's better. Look, sniff, taste, and stir from time to time, and see that the mixture doesn't get too dry. In which case add coffee in preference to water.

This is a no-panic recipe, for the ingredients can be varied every which way. Furthermore, it will feed up to twelve if it's served over macaroni, rice, or corn chips. A BIG green salad is called for, as well as hard rolls and red wine.

Bean Dishes from Dried Beans

Dried bean cooking is for not-so-Poor Poets who don't shudder at utility bills. It is necessary for those who receive a sack of beans at Christmas.

So all the preceding canned bean dishes can be made from scratch although it takes longer. Cooking time is decreased somewhat if a spoonful of unseasoned meat tenderizer is added to the overnight soak.

Here, however, are two elegant dried bean dinners that must be made from scratch and then only if black beans can be located. A Mexican or Chinese grocer is the best target. Black beans look like little blobs of India ink; they have a strong and wild flavor; they cost anywhere from twenty cents to a dollar a pound. They require at least three hours' cooking and sometimes costly ingredients. But the final product is superb.

1 *pound black beans*	1 *ham hock or small ham*
1 *medium onion*	*bone*
½ *bay leaf*	3 *dashes Tabasco*
⅛ *teaspoon thyme*	½ *teaspoon salt*
1 *large stalk celery*	¼ *cup Jamaica rum*
2 *branches parsley*	1½ *pints cold sour cream*

Sort the beans (leave one white one in for good luck) and soak overnight. Drain, cover with fresh water, add the next 6 ingredients and simmer, covered, 2½ to 3 hours. Pick out the vegetables and ham hock and drain the beans, reserving the liquid. Thicken a cup of it with little kneaded butter-flour balls, and return it to the beans along with the Tabasco, salt, and rum. Reheat and serve with gobs of sour cream, French bread and butter, red wine, and an enormous green salad.

BLACK BEANS ৫ 12
WITH SMOKED MEATS

This variation on a Brazilian national dish is good for winding up the day, any day, or celebrating in the grand manner.

1 *pound black beans*
2 *pounds smoked meats (about equal parts of corned*
  beef, smoked sausage, smoked pork, smoked tongue,
  and bacon)
1 *large onion, chopped*
3 *green onions, chopped*
1 *clove garlic, mashed*
4 *tablespoons bacon fat or oil*
  dash of cayenne
  salt to taste

Check the beans for assorted rocks and weed seeds and soak overnight. Or cover the beans with cold water, bring to a boil and boil several minutes, then allow to stand for an hour. Drain the beans, cover with fresh water, and simmer for 2 hours. In the meantime, simmer meats in a separate pan.

Drain the meat, reserving some liquid for possible later use, should the final result seem dry; peel the tongue and slice it, along with the other meats. Add meat to beans and continue cooking slowly until the beans are soft enough that some of them can be mashed.

Now sauté the onions in the fat, add the garlic and cayenne, and mix with the beans. Taste for seasoning, and the dish is ready to serve. Piles of steamed rice is a must. Twelve persons can eat this in one day, or one person in twelve days.

Jamaica rum or strong black coffee added now and then during the cooking does not hinder the dish one bit.

Black beans are to be more than briefly noted—never ignored. In the Roman midnight observation that closed the three-day Lemuria, or entertainment of the dead, the head of the household walked barefoot through all his rooms, throwing black beans behind him. His chant, repeated nine times: "These I give and with these redeem myself and my family." Close behind followed ghosts, who quickly and silently picked up the beans and departed, not to return until the time appointed for the next Lemuria.

Peas

Here are three things to do with lentils or yellow split peas—one each for Thackeray's sailors in "Little Billee". Going to sea with beef, captain's biscuits, and pickled pork, they ate so well that, by the time they crossed the equator, there was nothing left but one split pea.

As to the recipes, which require many times more the one pea in the sailor's ration, the first is hot, the second hotter, and the third mild and gentle and rather sweet.

FAHSOULIA BEYTHA WATEFAH ♄ 4

This came back from Egypt along with a water buffalo hassock and a pile of floor cushions.

1 *pound lentils or split peas*
3 *large onions, chopped*
3 *tablespoons butter*
¼ *teaspoon turmeric*
¼ *teaspoon pepper*
½ *teaspoon allspice*
1 *teaspoon salt*
1 *large apple, chopped*

Soak the peas overnight, drain, add fresh water and cook until tender (about 30 minutes to an hour). Drain, but reserve some liquid. Brown the onions in butter, add the seasonings and stir well. Now dump in the chopped apple and cook and stir until the apple is tender. Mix well with the peas and reheat, adding a little liquid if necessary. Serve with rice as a main dish. This is also a good side dish with lamb, pork, or poultry.

DHALL CURRY ♄ 4–6

Be sure there are lots of rice and hard rolls or sesame crackers and wine to minimize the effect of being aflame. Or go easy on the cayenne.

½ *pound lentils or split peas*
½ *teaspoon salt*
3 *medium onions, chopped*
2 *green peppers, chopped, seeds removed*
2 *large cloves garlic, chopped*
1 *can green chillies, seeded and chopped*
2 *tablespoons butter*
1 *teaspoon curry powder (more is better, but watch it)*
  cayenne to taste

Soak the peas overnight, drain, add fresh water and salt and cook until tender. Drain, but reserve a little liquid. Sauté the vegetables briefly—they should be somewhat crisp. Stir in the curry powder and cayenne and mix everything together well. Simmer about ten minutes and serve with rice. Fried sausage is good with this.

D. A. R. LENTILS AND HONEY ℃ 4

1 *pound lentils or split peas*
6 *slices uncooked bacon, chopped*
1 *teaspoon salt*
¼ *teaspoon pepper*
1 *teaspoon dry mustard*
¼ *cup chutney*
½ *cup honey*

Soak the peas overnight, drain, add fresh water and salt and cook until tender. Mix all the ingredients, pour into a covered baking dish and bake 30 minutes in a slow oven—about 325°. Remove the cover and bake 30 minutes longer. Add a little of the reserve liquid if necessary. This smacks of the Middle West and Grant Wood and goes well with brown bread and cole slaw.

Rice

"They had best not stir the rice, though it sticks in the pot," was Cervantes' advice, and it holds true today. Another bit of wisdom, necessitated by modern food distribution methods, is that the cook know which rice is which.

Although most rice is available in packages with printed cooking directions, some markets carry rice (usually in 5- or 10-pound sacks) with only the variety name indicated. The Poor Poet is admonished to familiarize himself with variety and kind for, not only is rice considerably less expensive if purchased in larger quantities, but *kind* greatly affects both cooking method and use.

Long grain rice cooks more quickly than other white rice and the result is drier, with the grains tending to remain separate.

Steam long grain varieties in a heavy pan with tight-fitting lid. Use 1½ cups cold water for each cup rice, and ½ teaspoon salt, if desired. Cover, bring to a wild boil, then lower heat and simmer, still covered, about 20 minutes.

Both medium and short grain rice cook a little more slowly and the result is moister, with grains tending to stick together. This makes the rice easier to eat with chopsticks. When using these kinds of rice in dishes such as Paella and Risotto, more of the sauce is absorbed by the rice, so that it loses its characteristic flavor.

To cook these, put equal amounts of rice and cold water in a deep pan with a tight lid. Bring to a boil, turn very low, and simmer 3 minutes. Bring again to a boil, reduce heat and simmer about 20 minutes. Remove the pan from heat and allow to stand, with the cover still on, for 7 minutes.

Leftover rice can be refrigerated and reheated in the top of a double boiler with considerable success. However, hot rice cooked by the usual methods does not hold well if dinner is much delayed. Nevertheless, long grain rice can be held if it is cooked only 10 or 15 minutes, then transferred to a colander set in a covered pan with a little boiling water in the bottom. The rice will take an additional 20 to 30 minutes to steam done, and will hold successfully over boiling water for an hour or more.

Need for a second good trick often arises after the rice has been successfully steamed: several unexpected and very hungry poets arrive. The problem must be universal, for almost every area has a solution and every solution a different name. Among them:

PEAS AND RICE

Toss hot cooked peas with twice as much steamed rice, more or less, and a little butter. Stir in a sprinkling of chili teppin, seeded and crushed, to taste. This is especially good with ham or chicken or fried fish.

BEANS AND RICE

Substitute drained canned kidney or red beans for the peas in the above recipe, and omit the chili teppin. Sprinkle with parched sesame seeds.

This combination is a holiday dish in Japan; a sharecropper's dinner in the South; a standby recipe from the nuns of Guadalupe; and, near the Mediterranean, a somewhat color-conscious delight called Moors and Christians. The latter is made with black beans.

HOPPING JOHN

Drop a ham bone into the water in which the rice is cooking, later adding peas or beans as above. If the ham bone hasn't been too well gnawed previously, this makes a good main dish.

PILAF OMAR ଓ 4–6

Pre-dinner philosophizing has a way of going on until the jug is empty, or someone is sent out for more, and that is emptied, too. As noted above, rice steamed in the usual manner doesn't sit out this sort of socializing well. Not to say that pilaf can't be overcooked, but the results aren't so disastrous.

4 *tablespoons butter*
1½ *cups raw rice*
3 *cups hot chicken or meat broth*

Stir the butter and rice, constantly and patiently, over low heat until the rice is slightly browned. Dump the mixture into a casserole, pour over the hot broth and cover tightly. Bake for 30 minutes at 400°, then turn off the oven, give the rice a stir, and let it sit uncovered for 5 to 10 minutes longer.

PILAF JUSTINE ଓ 4–6

1½ *cups rice (or half and half rice and bulghor)*
1 *tablespoon olive oil*
½ *cup Greek olives*
2 *tablespoons capers*
3 *cups boiling water*

Combine rice, oil, olives, and capers in a casserole. Pour in the boiling water, cover and bake for 30 minutes at 400°, then turn off the oven, give the rice a stir, and let it sit uncovered for 5 or 10 minutes longer.

GRANT AVENUE FRIED RICE ೪ 4–6

2 *tablespoons salad oil*
1 *cup finely diced chicken, ham, or pork*
1 *cup thinly sliced vegetables (mushrooms, green onion,*
   celery, and/or green pepper)
2 *tablespoons soy sauce*
1 *egg, well beaten*
3 *cups cold cooked rice*

Fry the meat gently; add the vegetables, rice and soy sauce and cook and stir slowly for 10 minutes. Mix in the egg and continue the cooking-stirring process for another 5 minutes. Serve with additional soy sauce on the side.

Japanese fried rice is manufactured of the same ingredients, plus a little chopped raw spinach, but the rice isn't fried. Instead, the whole is simmered gently in chicken or fish stock for 15 minutes or so, the egg added just before serving.

NASI GORENG ೪ 4–6

The Dutch East Indies version of fried rice is an elegant dish on a hot day. A fried egg is plunked on top of each serving, with sweet pickles, chutney, and sliced tomato to set it off. Beer is in order.

2 *onions, chopped*
1 *clove garlic, minced*
3 *chili teppins, seeded and chopped*
4 *tablespoons salad oil*
1 *to 2 cups cooked ham, bacon, chicken, or pork, diced*
4 *cups cold cooked rice*

Fry onions, garlic, and peppers slowly in oil until the onion is lightly brown. Add the meat and cook and stir an additional 5 or so minutes. Toss in the rice and mix well, adding a little more oil if necessary. Heat well and serve.

RICE WITH GREEN CHILLIES ℃ 6

    3 cups cooked rice
    2 cups sour cream
    ½ pound mild Cheddar cheese, diced
    1 can green chillies, chopped
        salt

Combine all ingredients, pack in a buttered baking dish, and heat for 30 minutes at 350°.

TURTA ℃ 4–6

4 eggs   1 cup grated mild Cheddar
3 tablespoons olive oil   cheese
2 cups cooked rice   salt and pepper

Beat three of the eggs and then stir in the other ingredients. Pour into a buttered baking dish and top with the remaining beaten egg. Bake 45 minutes at 350°. Serve as is or with any Italian sauce.

RICE PALAESTRA ℃ 4–6

Attributed to the lovely slave who so prettily bent and wriggled her hips while stirring the pot. This is an excellent main dish that also goes well with chicken.

3 tablespoons butter   1½ cups raw rice
1 onion, chopped fine   3 cups chicken stock
1 clove garlic, minced   1½ teaspoons salt
4 lettuce leaves, shredded   pepper
1 small can sliced mush-   1 cup cooked peas
    rooms, undrained   1 or 2 pimientos, chopped
1 cup stewed tomatoes   ¼ cup raisins, plumped in
4 sausages, diced   hot water

Sauté the onion in butter. Add all but the last three ingredients, mix well, and pour into a casserole with a tight cover. Bake at 400° for a half hour. Toss in the peas, pimiento, and raisins just before serving.

RIJSTAFEL

For the really mad poet, who wants to celebrate in the grand manner, and who has the time, cash, energy, space, dishes—as well as enough hungry friends—the Javanese rijstafel.

It requires mountains of steamed rice and as many condiments and side dishes as can be manufactured, arranged on the table, piled on each plate of rice, and consumed. Fifty-boy rijstafel is considered acceptable in the East Indies, albeit overwhelming for studio entertaining. Ten or so bowls from the following list should be impressive enough. And have the cook in a swivet.

Called for also are beer (preferably dark and plentiful) and an abundance of paper napkins or small towels wrung out in warm water.

1. *Mango chutney*
2. *Grated coconut*
3. *Chopped orange peel*
4. *Chopped grapefruit peel*

5. *Chopped green onions*
6. *Chopped sweet green pepper*
7. *Diced pineapple*
8. *Chopped roasted peanuts*
9. *Raisins, scalded to plump, and drained*
10. *Fried bananas, dusted with brown sugar, cinnamon, and cloves*
11. *Hot pickled peppers*
12. *Watermelon pickles*
13. *Small tomatoes stuffed with cucumbers*
14. *Pickled eggs*
15. *Pickled cucumbers*
16. *Pickled fish*
17. *Meat Sambal: ground meat and liver, garlic, shredded coconut, and Sambal* to taste. Fry slowly and moisten with meat stock.*
18. *Fish Sambal: equal parts of fish and sweet potatoes, both thinly sliced and fried in oil with Sambal to taste*
19. *Fried chicken*
20. *Fried shrimp*
21. *Fried or boiled fish*
22. *Fried eggs with garlic and sliced tomatoes*
23. *Servendel: diced beef or pork mixed with shredded coconut, peanuts, salt, and hot sauce, and fried*
24. *Fish (i.e., codfish) croquettes*
25. *Sajourmenny: any vegetables cut in small strips and simmered in coconut milk, curry powder, garlic, and onion*
26. *Sambal**

Plain steamed rice or rijstafel, not forgetting that Gautama divided all of mankind into ten classifications, with Buddha first, the counterpart of hell tenth—and rice second.

* A recipe for Sambal is on page 168.

Macaronis

Macaronis range in size from hair-thin Oriental noodles to the broad Italian lasagne and fat manicotti. From the poet, who prefers alphabets, to the dreamer who chooses wheels or stars, there is a multitude of shapes. Add to this the wide range of flavors: spinach, tomato, carrot, onion, herbs and spices, powdered tea, pounded shrimp, eggs.

Poor Poets of the Far East were eating macaroni products in 5000 B.C. And today's Poor Poet, if he chose, might spend a lifetime of macaroni dinners without ever repeating the same recipe twice. Though he might suffer from obesity.

Here is a handful to start with.

SPAGHETTI WITH GREEN SAUCE   ∾ 6

  1 *pound spaghetti or vermicelli*
  6 *tablespoons olive oil*
  4 *cloves garlic*
  1 *cup (packed) chopped parsley and/or fresh basil*
  4 *tablespoons butter*
    Parmesan cheese

While the spaghetti is cooking (but not overcooking) in a cauldron of boiling salted water, concoct the sauce. Heat olive oil and simmer the finely chopped garlic until it is golden. Toss in the parsley or basil, and continue cooking for 2 or 3 minutes. Now sprinkle in some black pepper, and the sauce is ready.

Drain the spaghetti and then dump it into a warm bowl along with the butter and sauce. Mix with care and industry and serve topped with lots of grated cheese.

NOODLES IN BUTTER

1 *pound egg noodles, cooked*
3 *tablespoons butter*
1 *pound cottage cheese*
1 *egg yolk*
  salt to taste
1 *or 2 tablespoons poppy seed*

Melt butter in a heavy frying pan and sauté cooked noodles until golden brown. This calls for some watching and stirring dexterity, as the noodles should not be allowed to turn into a large pancake. Mix egg yolk and salt with cottage cheese, and pour over the noodles. Allow the mixture to heat throughout. Serve with a generous sprinkling of poppy seeds.

LAZANKI WITH COTTAGE CHEESE

For the Poor Poet who has meringue in mind, this is a fine way to use up three egg yolks.

1 *pound egg noodles, cooked*
1 *cup cottage cheese*
2 *tablespoons sugar*
3 *egg yolks*
2 *cups sour cream*
  salt to taste
½ *cup bread crumbs*

Mix cottage cheese, egg yolks, sour cream, sugar, and salt and then combine with the noodles in a well-buttered baking dish. Strew crumbs over the top, and possibly some dabs of butter. Bake at 475° for about 30 minutes.

NOODLES WITH ALMONDS AND SEEDS 4–6

This is good as a main dish, or an accompaniment to pot roast. For those who like them, the addition of a handful of raisins is in order.

64   BEANS, PEAS, RICE, ETC.

½ cup shredded almonds
½ pound noodles
4 tablespoons butter
2 tablespoons poppy seed

While the noodles are cooking (about 10 minutes) and draining, brown nuts in butter. Slip noodles into a warm bowl, pour over the butter, nuts, and poppy seed, stir once or twice, and that's it.

If dinner is delayed, the dish can be kept hot over boiling water.

NOODLES WITH HAM AND BUTTERMILK   ๛ 4

½ pound noodles
1¼ cups diced ham
1 onion
1 cup buttermilk
2 eggs
1 cup grated Cheddar cheese
1 teaspoon Worcestershire
   salt and pepper to taste

Cook and drain noodles and chop the onion. Combine eggs and Worcestershire with buttermilk. Now, with all ingredients at hand, and a buttered baking dish for a base, begin making layers of noodles, ham, onion, cheese, and buttermilk-egg. Sprinkle intermittently with salt and pepper. When the building process is completed, cover the dish and bake for 30 minutes at 375°. Uncover and bake for an additional 15 minutes.

My great aunt's Cousin Carrie, who passed this recipe on to me, advised using chopped cabbage if there was no ham to be had. She further noted that a combination of chopped apples and raisins was another substitute that she liked a lot.

½ pound noodles
2 packages cream cheese or ½ pint cottage cheese
1 small can chopped black olives
4 tablespoons butter
½ teaspoon crushed basil

Put cooked and drained noodles and butter in a low oven or over boiling water while combining the cheese, olives, and basil. Toss everything gently but thoroughly, allow to heat well, and the dish is ready to serve.

FALSE RAVIOLI ♋ 6

These ravioli have no outsides. They may be splashed with meat or tomato sauce as a dish in themselves, or used with both spaghetti and sauce for a more generous feast. Or—the mixture may be used for stuffing mani-cotti. See below.

2 cups chopped cooked spinach
1 cup ricotta cheese
½ cup grated Parmesan cheese
2 eggs
  salt and pepper to taste
  flour

Measure all ingredients into a large bowl. Using hands, mix everything well and shape into small balls. Roll these in flour and then drop into boiling salted water. Simmer for 20 minutes, drain, and serve.

Manicotti, which freely translated means "little muffs", are large, thin-walled tubes of macaroni. Simmer manicotti as directed on the package and stuff with uncooked False Ravioli. Lay these in an oiled baking dish, top with meat or tomato sauce, and bake 20 minutes at 350°.

MR. MUSCETTI'S TURKEY DRESSING

Sufficient to stuff a 20-pound turkey, this dressing may also be used to fill manicotti, layer with lasagne, or (and this was the original intention) make real homemade ravioli.

1 *beef brain, parboiled and chopped*
1 *pound ground veal*
1 *pound ground pork*
  olive oil
2 *pounds spinach or Swiss chard, parboiled and chopped*
3 *cloves garlic, chopped*
3 *stalks celery, chopped*
1 *medium onion, chopped*
2 *tablespoons chopped parsley*
⅛ *teaspoon each ground allspice, cloves, cinnamon, and poultry seasoning*
5 *eggs*
1 *cup grated Parmesan cheese*
½ *cup grated bread*
  salt and pepper to taste

Heat a little olive oil in a large frying pan and brown veal and pork lightly. Blend in spinach, garlic, celery, parsley, and onion. Add the chopped brain and spices, and cook for several minutes. Turn the mixture into a large bowl and allow to cool slightly. Then, using a big wooden spoon, beat in the eggs, one at a time. Toss in cheese and bread, and beat a little more. If the mixture seems too dry, another egg or two will remedy the matter, and the stuffing is ready to be used as desired.

SPAGHETTI SAUCE   ↻ 6–8

Start this spaghetti sauce at the break of a cold and dreary day. (In northern latitudes, arise an hour earlier.) Simmer it on and off as the weather continues or worsens. Stir and taste occasionally, adding more wine if the sauce becomes too thick. And, in the evening, with a blustery wind invading any crack, serve it over a platter of steaming spaghetti.

3 or 4 *large cloves garlic*	1 *can tomato paste*
2 *medium onions*	$\frac{1}{4}$ *teaspoon sugar*
4 *tablespoons olive oil*	1 *teaspoon salt*
1 *pound lean ground beef*	$\frac{1}{4}$ *teaspoon cayenne*
$\frac{1}{2}$ *cup chopped celery*	1 *teaspoon each rosemary,*
1 *cup dry red wine*	*basil, thyme, and*
1 *large can solid pack*	*oregano*
tomatoes	

Chop garlic and onions and sauté in oil until golden. Add ground beef and cook and stir with a fork until meat is brown. Drop in all other ingredients, in any order; lower heat; cover and simmer for several hours, at least, or preferably as noted above.

ONE POTS

The fine One Pot has innumerable advantages inherent in its name: the dishwasher, who often doubles as cook, is saved for future culinary orgies; the necessity of purchasing an extra dish for serving is eliminated; the dish itself is easy on both the budget and chef; and, a One Pot may be carried to the home of an ailing friend, to the park, or to a church social.

Except for an occasional stir and taste during cooking, the One Pot requires little attention. However, there *are* two rules: never use weary vegetables; never allow the contents to boil.

One Pots That Require No Meat

The stability of produce prices is comparable to that of an artistic temperament. Thus, the dishes that appear first on the assumption that they are least extravagant, might—during a period of inclement weather and bad crops—prove to be exorbitant. Then again, all ingredients for the last dish might just be discovered the day the refrigerator is defrosted: bonus dinner.

But here's one relatively unaffected by defrosting or season, though it tastes best on a cold night.

A RAGOUT OF ONIONS

4 *large onions*
4 *tablespoons butter*
½ *cup gravy or bouillon*
¼ *teaspoon dry mustard*
   salt and pepper to taste

Peel and slice onions, separating rings. Cook in butter, stirring to prevent sticking. When the onions are soft and golden add the gravy into which the mustard has been blended. Season with salt and pepper and stir gently until the ragout is thick. Serve to two along with thick slabs of dark rye bread and butter, a green salad, and red wine.

ELK RIVER STEW 4-6

6 *potatoes*
1 *large onion*
2 *tablespoons butter*
½ *cup cream*

½ *cup milk*
   salt and pepper
6 *pilot crackers*

Slice the potatoes and onion and cook together in water to cover. When the vegetables are done stir in the butter, cream, milk, and seasonings. Serve with pilot crackers and a vegetable salad.

POTATO DEUTSCHER

7 *potatoes*
6 *slices stale bread*
2 *eggs*
1 *teaspoon salt*

pepper
2 *cups milk*
1 *cup sour cream*

Grate the potatoes, rinse in cold water and press dry. Soak bread in milk, beat in eggs and seasonings, and then stir in the potatoes. Pour into a buttered dish, top with sour cream, and bake at 350° for 45 minutes.

VEGETABLES IN GARLIC
AND OLIVE OÏL   ℃ 6

4 *cloves garlic, minced*
¼ *cup olive oil*
4 *large onions, sliced thin*
4 *green peppers, quartered, seeds removed*
1 *large eggplant, sliced thin*
6 *medium zucchini squash, sliced*
6 *tomatoes, sliced*
½ *cup grated Parmesan cheese*
　 salt and pepper

Build this dish in a covered earthenware casserole.

Sauté half the garlic in olive oil. On top of this add, in the order given above, the layers of vegetables, separating the eggplant and zucchini with the remaining garlic, and sprinkling each layer with salt and pepper. Strew the cheese over the top, sprinkle with a few drops of olive oil, and cover tightly. Cook over low heat for 30 minutes. If too much liquid develops, cook uncovered for the last few minutes. Serve with French bread and butter.

PETER'S PEPPER STEW   ℃ 4

3 *large onions*   3 *or 4 tomatoes*
1 *clove garlic*   3 *large potatoes*
4 *tablespoons olive oil*   1 *teaspoon marjoram leaves*
5 *large green peppers*   　 *salt and pepper*
2 *green chili peppers*

Sauté the onion, cut into large chunks, and the minced garlic in olive oil until they are limp and golden. Cut the vegetables in generous pieces, being sure to omit any trace of pepper seeds, which can prove unbearably hot. Now add the vegetables to the pot, along with the seasonings, cover and cook 45 minutes, or until the potatoes are tender. Check intermittently to see that the pot does not become too dry, and stir with caution. Serve the stew in earthenware bowls and accompanied by crusty bread and butter.

RED CABBAGE WITH WINE ♋ 2–4

This dish, along with mashed potatoes or potato pancakes, makes a good cold night dinner. One or two bouillon cubes dissolved in the hot water make for a richer dish.

1 *head red cabbage*
  red wine vinegar
1 *tablespoon butter or bacon fat*
1 *tablespoon brown sugar*
1 *teaspoon salt*
  pepper to taste and a dash of nutmeg
1 *onion, finely chopped*
1 *or 2 apples, finely chopped*
1 *tablespoon vinegar*
1 *cup red wine*
  cloves or caraway seeds (optional)
¼ *cup currant jelly*

Slice the cabbage and soak in red wine vinegar mixed with equal parts of water for 30 minutes. Melt the butter in a saucepan and add the drained cabbage along with the sugar, salt, pepper, nutmeg, and onion. Cover and simmer for 20 minutes or until the cabbage begins to appear a little dry, lifting the lid every so often to stir. Add one cup hot water, the red wine, vinegar, and chopped apple. A few cloves or caraway seeds may be tossed in now. Cover and let cook slowly until tender—about 25 minutes. Just before serving stir in the currant jelly.

MATTER-PANEER   ℃ 4

1 *onion, sliced thin*
2 *tablespoons butter*
1 *10-ounce package frozen
   peas*
1 *teaspoon salt*
¾ *teaspoon curry powder*

¾ *teaspoon turmeric*
2 *mint leaves (if possible)*
1 *pint large curd cottage
   cheese, well drained*
¼ *teaspoon chili powder*

Sauté the onions in butter until soft. Blend in the curry powder and turmeric. Add the peas, salt, and mint leaves. Cover and cook 5 to 8 minutes, or until the peas are just tender. Just before serving blend in the cottage cheese and chili powder. Let stand a few minutes to heat through, but don't continue cooking or the cottage cheese will melt.

Sliced tomatoes with cracked pepper, and corn or sesame seed crackers go with this.

CORN PUDDING   ℃ 6

Just (almost, anyway) like mother used to make.

1 *one-pound can cream-style corn*
1 *to 1½ cups any or all of the following: diced celery,
   chopped ripe olives, onions, pimiento, or green pepper*
1 *tablespoon butter*
2 *eggs*
1 *teaspoon salt*
¼ *teaspoon each pepper and dry mustard*
½ *teaspoon paprika or chili powder*
½ *cup cracker crumbs, crushed cornflakes, or grated
   Parmesan cheese*

Melt the butter in an earthenware pot and simmer the mixed vegetables (except the corn) gently. Beat eggs slightly and add to the pot along with the corn and seasonings. Mix well. Sprinkle crumbs or cheese over the top and bake for 45 minutes at 350°.

TORTILLAS WITH
TOMATO CREAM   ℭ 2–3

 6 *corn tortillas*
   oil for frying
 ½ *pound Jack cheese*
 1 *4-ounce can peeled green chili peppers*
 1 *onion*
 1 *clove garlic*
 1½ *cups tomato purée*
 1 *teaspoon each salt and oregano*
 1 *pint sour cream*

Fry the tortillas lightly (but see that they remain
limp). Place strips of cheese and chili pepper on each,
roll, and place in a baking pan. Chop the onion and garlic
and brown in the same oil. Drain excess oil, add the
tomato purée and seasonings, and simmer covered for
30 minutes. Blend in the sour cream. Pour this sauce
over the tortillas, cover and bake 30 minutes at 350°.

A PORTUGUESE PANCAKE   ℭ 6

 2 *pounds zucchini squash*
 1 *large onion*
 1 *green pepper*
 1 *or 2 cloves garlic*
 2 *or 3 sprigs each parsley and celery tops*
 5 *tablespoons olive oil*
 1 *8-ounce tin tomato sauce or 2 large tomatoes*
 1 *teaspoon each basil and oregano*
 5 *eggs*
 ½ *cup milk*
 ½ *cup grated cheese*
   salt, pepper, and paprika

Use a heavy frying pan with a lid. Dice the vegetables and brown quickly in the olive oil. Add tomato sauce or tomatoes, basil and oregano, and simmer until the mixture is barely moist. Beat eggs with milk and a little salt and pepper, and pour over the vegetables. Cover and cook until the eggs begin to set. Sprinkle with cheese and paprika and brown under the broiler. Serve in pie-shaped wedges.

One Pots with Meat

JAGER KOHL ∾ 4

½ *pound bacon or sausages*
2 *or 3 large potatoes*
1 *small head cabbage*
2 *tablespoons flour*
   salt, cracked pepper, and cider vinegar to taste
½ *pint sour cream or yogurt*

Fry the bacon in a frying pan with lid. Drain off most of the fat and add thick slices of peeled potatoes and cabbage. Sprinkle flour over the vegetables, add water to barely cover, along with salt and a dash of vinegar. Cover and cook slowly 45 minutes to an hour. Serve along with a bowl of sour cream, cracked pepper, and a little cruet of vinegar for those who like a sharper flavor. Rye bread and butter and a salad of apples and raisins rounds out this meal.

LOUISE'S DUTCH DISH

"Potatoes is the best vegetable," declares a very young friend. And here is another One Pot based on that "best vegetable".

To figure out how much of what to use, multiply the

following ingredients by the number of persons sitting hungrily by. An ample Dutch Dish for one requires:

1 *each small onion, apple, and potato*
2 *or 3 slices bacon*
   pepper

Fry the bacon, but do not allow it to get crisp. In the meantime, peel and grate the vegetables and apple. Break up the bacon, drain off a little fat, add the vegetables and fry gently until everything is done. Turn out on a hot plate and grind lots of pepper over the top. Eat as is or with fried eggs . . . and hot, strong coffee.

HOG AND HOMINY   ७ 2–3

¾ *pound bacon, ham, or sausages*
2 *tablespoons butter*
1 *#2½ can hominy*
½ *cup milk*
1 *teaspoon paprika*
¼ *teaspoon salt*

Use a frying pan with lid. Cut up the meat and sauté in butter. Move the meat to the center of the pan, pour drained hominy around, sprinkle with paprika and salt, and add the milk. Cover and simmer 5 or 10 minutes, or until all the milk is absorbed.

Hog and Hominy presents possibilities. Green onions can be sautéed with the meat. Chili powder can replace the paprika. Or the milk can be increased to a cup or more, and a teaspoon of gumbo filé powder mixed in just before serving. In this case bowls, not plates, for eating. Furthermore, the name can be changed to protect the delicate.

POCKET-POOR   ℃ 4

2½ *pounds sweet onions*
1½ *pounds potatoes*
¾ *cup rice*
½ *pound smoked sausages*
 salt, cracked pepper, and cider vinegar to taste

Peel potatoes, slice thick, and bring to a boil in water just to cover. Add the onions, which are also in thick slices, rice, and cut-up sausages. Season with a little salt, cover, and simmer slowly for about 30 minutes. Just before serving sprinkle a little cider vinegar and freshly cracked pepper over the dish. A vegetable salad with a mild sour cream or yogurt dressing goes well, as does rye or pumpernickel bread with lots of butter.

TIN CAN SPECIAL   ℃ 4

Even the poet with such limited equipment as a frying pan, knife, and spoon can put together this dish.

2 *medium onions*
 butter
1 *#2 can corned beef hash*
1 *#2 can baked beans*
1 *#2 can tomatoes, drained*
4 *eggs*

Slice the onions and sauté them in butter until golden. Empty the tins into the frying pan and stir well. Put the pan into a 375° oven and bake until brown. Break the eggs on top of the hash and return to oven until done.

PEASANT POTATOES   ℧ 6–8

> 6 *boiled potatoes*
> 3 *hard-cooked eggs*
> 1 *teaspoon salt*
> 1 *cup sour cream*
> 1 *cup diced ham or smoked sausage*
> ½ *cup bread crumbs*
> 2 *tablespoons melted butter*
> ½ *cup heavy cream*

Slice the potatoes and eggs and combine in a buttered baking dish with the salt, sour cream, and ham. Pour cream over the top and sprinkle with the crumbs that have been mixed with butter. Bake 30 minutes at 450°.

POTATO SALAD—OVEN METHOD   ℧ 6

Back again is the "best vegetable", found now in a dish that is just fine for a rained-out picnic.

> 6 *cups sliced cooked potatoes*
> 2 *teaspoons salt*
>   *pepper*
> ½ *teaspoon celery salt*
> ¼ *cup each cider vinegar and salad oil*
> 1 *teaspoon prepared mustard*
> ¼ *cup minced onions*
> 6 *frankfurters*

Combine everything but the frankfurters in a baking dish and allow to marinate for at least half an hour. Cut the frankfurters diagonally into 2-inch pieces and tuck well into the potatoes. Bake, covered, for 30 minutes at 350°. Uncover, and allow to bake an additional 10 minutes.

SAUSAGES WITH YAMS
AND APPLES

ᶜ 6

Designed for the first crisp autumn day.

2 *large yams or sweet potatoes*
3 *large cooking apples*
1 *pound bulk or link pork sausage*
⅔ *cup brown sugar*
½ *teaspoon salt*

Boil, peel, and slice the yams and core and slice the apples. If using bulk sausage, make 6 patties. Brown sausage in skillet and set aside. Drain most of the fat from the pan and then lay in it alternate layers of yams and apples. Sprinkle each layer with brown sugar and salt. Top with the sausage, cover, and bake 30 minutes at 350°. Remove the cover and bake until the apples are soft.

Cole slaw is a good companion. So is cranberry sauce. And so, too, hot corn bread with lots of butter.

GREEN PEA PIE

ᶜ 6

1 9-*inch unbaked pastry shell*
8 *slices bacon*
2 *medium onions*
1 10-*ounce package frozen peas, partially defrosted*
4 *eggs*
1½ *cups milk*
1 *teaspoon salt*
¼ *teaspoon hickory smoked salt*
⅛ *teaspoon pepper*

Dice, fry, and drain the bacon. Pour off all but about ¼ cup drippings and in this sauté the thinly sliced onions until limp. Layer onions, bacon, and peas in pastry shell.

Beat the other ingredients and pour over. Bake in the lower part of a 400° oven for 40 to 45 minutes, or until the custard is set.

10-MINUTE HAM AND GREEN BEANS   ↢ 4–6

This is really a two-pot, but because it's so speedy to put together it's been sneaked into the One Pot category.

2 cups cooked cubed ham
1 tablespoon drippings
1 10-ounce package frozen
   green beans, cooked
   tender-crisp
1 4-ounce can water
   chestnuts

1 tablespoon butter
1 tablespoon flour
½ cup milk
½ cup sour cream
1 tablespoon soy sauce
⅓ cup cracker crumbs
4 tablespoons melted butter

Haul out the frying pan that can double as baking and serving dish. In it brown the ham and pour off any drippings before adding the green beans and water chestnuts, drained and thinly sliced. Leave pan over low heat. In pot number two melt 1 tablespoon butter. Stir in the flour and add the milk. Cook, stirring constantly, until mixture thickens. Add the sour cream and soy sauce, mix well, and then pour over ham and vegetables. Sprinkle crumbs and melted butter over all. Place the dish under the broiler for 2 or 3 minutes, or until the crumbs are lightly browned.

SAFARI SQUASH   ↢ 4

2 small acorn squash or
1 small pumpkin
1½ cups bouillon
½ pound lean ground beef
1 cup rice
2 tablespoons butter

1 chili teppin
1 teaspoon curry powder
½ cup yogurt
1 bay leaf
½ teaspoon ground cloves

Steam the squash for about 20 minutes, or until just tender. Cool, cut in half lengthwise, and scoop out the seeds. (If a pumpkin is used, steam, cook, but leave whole, merely scooping seeds out from the top jack-o-lantern style.) In the meantime cook the beef in the bouillon and drain, reserving the stock. Brown the rice in butter. Add a little salt, the crumbled chili teppin, and one cup of stock. Simmer, covered, until rice is done. Add curry powder, yogurt, and ground beef and stuff the squash with this mixture. Bake for an hour at 350°, basting occasionally with the remaining stock to which the crushed bay leaf and cloves have been added.

SWEET-SOUR PORK ༒ 4

1 *pound lean pork shoulder or leftover pork roast fat or oil*

1 *cup bouillon*

3 *teaspoons soy sauce pepper to taste*

2 *large green peppers*

1 *medium onion*

4 *slices pineapple (or equivalent chunk-style)*

3 *tablespoons cornstarch*

$\frac{1}{4}$ *cup cider vinegar*

$\frac{1}{4}$ *cup sugar*

$\frac{1}{2}$ *cup pineapple syrup*

Cut the pork in $\frac{1}{2}$-inch cubes and thoroughly brown in a little fat. Sprinkle with 1 teaspoon soy sauce and a little pepper, pour on the bouillon, and cook very gently, covered, for 20 minutes. (If leftover pork roast is used, heat only to bring the bouillon to a boil.) Cut the green peppers and onions in wedges, add, along with the pineapple pieces, and allow to cook uncovered for 5 minutes. In the meantime, blend the cornstarch, sugar, vinegar, 2 teaspoons soy sauce, and syrup, and add to the above. Cook no longer than 5 additional minutes, stirring all the time. Remember that the vegetables must remain crisp. Serve with steamed rice.

PACIFIC PORK AND CABBAGE 4

1 *pound lean pork shoulder*
  fat or oil
1 *cup diced onion*
1½ *pounds cabbage*
4 *teaspoons soy sauce*
  salt and pepper to taste

Cut the pork in thin strips and brown in a little fat. Pile in the onions and shredded cabbage. Stir over high heat for 3 to 5 minutes. Add soy sauce and a little salt and pepper. Cover and continue to cook for 1 or 2 minutes—the vegetables *must* remain crisp. Serve over hot noodles, and additional soy sauce on the side.

CARBONADO 4–6

2 *large onions*
2 *tablespoons fat*
1 *pound ground beef*
1 *large tomato*
½ *cup bouillon*

3 *large potatoes*
3 or 4 *apples or firm*
  peaches
½ *cup raisins*
  salt and pepper

Chop onions and sauté until golden. Add the meat and allow to brown. Stir and crumble the meat with a fork while the browning is progressing. Now add the peeled and cut-up tomato along with the bouillon. Cover and cook slowly 15 minutes. During this interval peel the potatoes and apples and slice them very thin. Now lay them on top of the meat, season with a little salt and pepper, and replace the lid. Simmer until the potatoes are done. Add the raisins about 5 minutes before removing from the fire. It's not at all a bad idea to check every so often, for if it's allowed to dry there is a serious shrinkage problem.

RATATOUILLE, NON-CLASSICAL STYLE

1 *medium eggplant*
2 *onions*
1 *can stewed tomatoes*
1 *bay leaf*
½ *teaspoon brown sugar*
½ *pound lean ground beef*
   olive oil
   salt and pepper

Soak peeled and diced eggplant in salt water for an hour. Then boil until tender with the onions, chopped, crushed bay leaf, and a little salt and pepper. Brown the meat in olive oil and then add to the eggplant-onion mixture along with the stewed tomatoes and brown sugar. Heat well, or better yet, refrigerate overnight, then heat and serve with steamed rice and a dish of cold yogurt.

END-OF-MONTH STROGANOFF

4 *ounces noodles*
¾ *cup sliced onions*
1 *pound ground beef*
   fat or oil
¼ *cup flour*
¾ *teaspoon salt*
   dash pepper
¼ *cup tomato sauce or*
   catsup
1 *teaspoon Worcestershire*
1 *bouillon cube*
1 *8-ounce can mushroom*
   pieces, with liquid
1⅓ *cups buttermilk*

Cook noodles and drain. Meanwhile brown the onions and ground beef in a little fat. Remove from the fire and blend in the flour, salt, and pepper. Crumble the bouillon cube and add, along with all other ingredients, and mix everything well. Now stir in the noodles, turn the mixture into a buttered baking dish, and bake for 25 to 30 minutes at 350°.

E-O-M Stroganoff is obviously portable, making it fine for picnics in the back yard or longer pilgrimages. Purists, however, might prefer to serve the stroganoff over the noodles (or rice) and skip the business about the oven.

MEAT BALLS WITH PEAS AND CURRY   ℧ 6–8

Here we have a One Pot with just a hint of curry. Poor Poets addicted to this spice are urged to proceed at their own discretion.

1½ *pounds ground beef*
¾ *cup bread crumbs*
1 *cup tomato juice*
1 *egg*
½ *cup minced onion*
2 *teaspoons salt*
  pepper
  fat or oil
————
2 *tablespoons butter*

⅓ *cup chopped onion*
⅓ *cup chopped celery*
3 *tablespoons flour*
1 *tablespoon curry powder*
1 *teaspoon salt*
⅛ *teaspoon ground cloves*
2 *cups milk*
1 *10-ounce package frozen peas, partially defrosted juice of* ½ *lemon*

Make meat balls from the first list of ingredients, brown in a little fat, and set aside. In the same pan melt 2 tablespoons butter and sauté the onion and celery for a few minutes. Blend in flour, curry powder, cloves, and salt. Add the milk and cook, stirring steadily, until thickened and smooth. Beware: if the sauce is allowed to boil it will no doubt separate.

Now plop in the peas, meat balls, and lemon juice and stir to blend. Cook on top of stove 8 to 10 minutes or bake 10 to 15 minutes at 350°. Serve with steamed rice and a big green salad.

UP-COUNTRY MEAT BALLS
AND VEGETABLES

What, meat balls again? And why not. The puppy
has been put on a hamburger diet, and it is both con-
venient and permissible to rob from his supply.

2 *pounds ground beef*	½ *teaspoon marjoram*
1 *egg*	8 *each small carrots, small*
1½ *teaspoons salt*	*white onions, small*
¼ *teaspoon pepper*	*potatoes*
dash Worcestershire	*fat or oil*
½ *cup dry red wine or*	3 *or 4 big fresh*
water	*mushrooms*
2 *cans beef gravy (or one*	1 *tablespoon butter*
can gravy and one can	*chopped parsley*
red wine)	

Mix the first 8 ingredients, make eight or so generous
meat balls, and brown in hot fat. Remove to a baking
dish. Peel vegetables, leave whole, and cook for about
15 minutes in boiling salted water, then add them to
the meat balls. Add gravy and marjoram to the pan in
which the meat balls cooked, bring to a boil, and pour
over the meat and vegetables. Cover and bake 1 hour
at 350°.

When ready to serve, arrange mushroom slices that
have been browned in butter, and the chopped parsley,
over the dish.

MEATS

Poor Poets, unless they truly are vegetarians, need meat. It is all well and good to claim that 10 slices of fortified bread will give one the same energy value as a pound of lean beef, or that there are as many calories in three martinis, including the olive, as there are in a fine fillet. Or is it?

Poor Poets need meat because it is better for them than suppers of fortified bread and martinis. They need meat because it is good for them to say, "I had steak for dinner last night," and mean it because it is true.

There are skills to eating meat every (or almost every) night and still maintaining a handful of spare change. And the main one is to let the "weekend specials", not the palate, be the deciding factor in what to eat when. Also important is possession of a good sharp knife and the ability to use it. This latter comes with lots of initial nerve and continued practice. For those weekend specials usually come as is, and any custom cutting required of the butcher will considerably inflate the cost. A good boning knife is really a must, and it's worth one's while to prowl the used hardware stores for one.

There is, nonetheless, the fable of the Poor Poet who spent so much on cutlery that he was condemned to an extended diet of day-old bread and the like.

Heed the message.

Beef

Start with a functional blade chuck roast. Which means four distinct and different meat meals, *not* an enormous Sunday pot roast followed by a week of warmed-overs.

Using the best knife the budget will allow, cut away the strip of meat next to the blade and including the surface on which the grade is stamped. Roll this, with the surface side out, tie with stout string, and there is meal number one: rolled roast.

Next, work on the opposite side, removing the bony edge (but leaving some meat). This is the second meal, which might be a stew or a thick soup.

Exposed now is an oval boneless area. Cut or pull this away and slice for steaks. The flavor is as good as that of the most expensive, and tenderness is guaranteed if a sprinkling of tenderizer is used just before cooking. Another good tenderizing technique is to poke holes in the meat and then give it a generous olive oil bath. And there are others: lemon juice, red wine, beer.

On to meal number four, which now remains on the cutting board: pot roast.

POT ROAST WITH HONEY AND LEMON   ও 4

Here's a pot roast method that results in good sandwiches if the initial dish is served to two instead of the four indicated.

2 *pounds beef cut for pot roast*
1 *teaspoon garlic salt*
1 *teaspoon paprika*
1 *or 2 tablespoons flour*
1 *or 2 tablespoons shortening*

1 *tablespoon lemon juice and a slice of rind*
1 *tablespoon honey*
1 *bouillon cube*
½ *cup water*
1 *small onion, chopped*

Rub the beef with salt, paprika, and flour and brown well in hot shortening. Add the remaining ingredients, cover and let simmer until meat is tender. This will take almost 2 hours. The meat saved for sandwiches should be allowed to cool in the liquid unless the latter has been all used up for gravy.

POT ROAST IN PALANQUIN ෬ 4

2 *pounds beef cut for pot roast*
½ *package dehydrated onion soup mix*
½ *cup red wine*
heavy aluminum foil

Here the aluminum palanquin seals in all the juices and flavor and makes a fine substitute Dutch oven.

Place the beef on a generous piece of foil, sprinkle with onion soup mix, turn up the edges of the foil a bit, and add the wine. Now wrap the meat securely but not too tightly. Lay the palanquin on a baking pan or additional sheet of foil. Bake at 350° for 2 hours. This is good with mashed potatoes, for there is lots of rich brown juice.

POT ROAST WITH CRUMBS ෬ 4 or 5

This is pretty close to a One Pot for the end result is a pot roast surrounded by a rich bread pudding laced with wine and vegetables.

2 to 2½ *pounds beef cut for pot roast*
1 *clove garlic, mashed*
1 *cup dry bread crumbs*
¾ *pound carrots, sliced*
¼ *pound mushrooms, sliced*
¼ *cup sliced green olives*
½ *sweet red pepper, diced*
1 *fresh pig's foot*
2 *cups dry red table wine*
   a bouquet garni of parsley, bay, and thyme

Sear the meat in a little fat and sprinkle it with garlic. Surround with the other ingredients, topping with the pig's foot and bouquet garni. Cover the pot tightly, preferably sealing the lid with flour-water paste. Simmer slowly for 2 to 2½ hours, or cook for the same amount of time in a 350° oven.

GARLIC ROLLED ROAST   ∾ 4

2 *pounds beef cut for rolling*
2 *or 3 cloves of garlic, mashed*
   olive oil and red wine vinegar

Before rolling the roast, rub with olive oil and a very little red wine vinegar. Then spread with mashed garlic. Roll, tie, and wrap in waxed paper, and allow to stand for several hours.

Brown the roast (remove the paper first, please) in a 500° oven for about 20 minutes. Then lower heat to 300° and continue cooking, allowing 25 to 40 minutes per pound.

ROLLED ROAST, SAUERBRATEN STYLE

ↄ 4

2 *pounds beef, cut for rolling*
4 *tablespoons dry red wine*
2 *tablespoons tarragon vinegar*
½ *teaspoon salt*
½ *teaspoon pepper*
 dash each thyme, mace, sage, allspice, mustard, and cloves
½ *bay leaf, crushed*
1 *small onion*
1 *small carrot*
sprig of celery

Chop vegetables and combine all ingredients. Then generously slather this mixture over the meat. Roll, with the fat side out, and tie. Wrap the roast in waxed paper and allow it to stand for several hours at room temperature, or overnight in the refrigerator. The longer it stands, up to a point that is, the more distinct will be the sauerbraten flavor.

Roast as in preceding recipe. Potato pancakes go with this.

ROLLED ROAST DAUPHINE

ↄ 4

2 *to* 2½ *pounds rolled roast*
1 *or* 2 *tablespoons shortening*
½ *cup each sliced carrots and onions*
½ *teaspoon each thyme and marjoram leaves*
½ *bay leaf, crushed*
2 *big tablespoons chopped parsley*
4 *or* 5 *peppercorns*
1½ *cups dry red wine*
¾ *cup Madeira wine*
1 *cup reconstituted chicken or veal gravy mix*

Dry the meat well with paper towels and sear in very hot fat along with the chopped vegetables and herbs. Lower the heat slightly and slosh the red wine over the meat, allowing the juices to become syrupy. Now pour over the Madeira and gravy and allow to come to a boil on top of the stove. Next put the roast into a 250° oven and cook for a half to three-quarters of an hour, basting frequently.

The center cut of the chuck roast, usually reserved for steaks, can also be treated in this manner. In which case the dish becomes Beef Dauphine.

The building of a good stew is to be reserved for a cold day. Dishes in this genre usually improve themselves by sitting on the back of the stove for many hours. Then, just before serving they are brought to a steaming bubbliness.

Avoid the insidious grey-beige stew: thoroughly dry each piece of meat with paper toweling; brown the meat in very hot fat, and don't crowd it in the pan. A task that can prove hot and smoky but one that guarantees a rich brown triumph.

PARRIKA BEEF　　　　　　　　　　ひ 6

2 *pounds beef cut for stew*　　1 *teaspoon salt*
1 *tablespoon oil*　　　　　　　4 *tablespoons paprika*
1 *pound onions*　　　　　　　　1 *teaspoon wine vinegar*
1 *teaspoon caraway seeds*　　　1 *cup dry red wine*
½ *teaspoon marjoram*

Brown the meat well and set aside. In the meantime, slice onions as thin as possible and sauté until golden. Add caraway seeds, marjoram, salt, and paprika. Stir well and moisten with vinegar. Now return the meat to the pan, add wine, cover tightly, and simmer for about 2 hours. If the dish tends to get too dry, add a little water from time to time. Serve Paprika Beef with buttered noodles. A salad that includes beets and a few tarragon leaves is good to round out the dinner.

STELLA'S BEEF WITH PICKLED ONIONS ♋ 4–6

2 *pounds beef cut for stew*
1 *tablespoon oil*
2 *one-pound cans stewed tomatoes*
4 *peppercorns*
2 *whole cardamom seeds or* 1 *bay leaf*
½ *cup pickled onions, with juice*
salt to taste

Brown the beef and add peppercorns, cardamom seeds, salt, and stewed tomatoes. Cover and simmer about 2 hours, or until the meat is tender. Pour in the onions and search for the peppercorns and cardamom seeds. Remove these. This stew definitely calls for mashed potatoes.

BEEF STEW WITH WATER CHESTNUTS ♋ 4

¼ *pound salt pork*
1½ *pounds beef cut for stew*
1 *large clove garlic*
1 *large onion*
1 *cup bouillon*
1 *can tomato sauce*
1 *tablespoon pickling spices*
6 *peppercorns*
3 *potatoes*
1 *small can water chestnuts*
½ *teaspoon salt*

Dice the salt pork and brown in a heavy pan. Next brown the stew meat, and then the garlic and onion that has been sliced thin. Move this to a baking dish along with the bouillon, tomato sauce, and spices tied in cheesecloth. Cover and bake 1½ hours at 350°. Now add the potatoes, peeled and sliced, and the water chestnuts, drained and sliced thin. Sprinkle with salt. Re-cover and bake an additional 45 minutes.

BEEF IN RUM ↻ 4–6

A celebration feast for the not-so-Poor Poet, who must not shirk on any of the ingredients.

2 *pounds beef cut for stew*
¼ *cup Jamaica rum*
2 *tablespoons butter*
2 *tablespoons flour*
1 *teaspoon salt*
1 *tablespoon catsup*
1 *tablespoon currant jelly*

1 *tablespoon wine vinegar*
1 *bay leaf*
2 *cups water*
2 *cups sliced fresh mushrooms*
½ *cup chopped parsley*

Sprinkle half the rum over the meat and let stand for several hours (overnight is better). Brown the meat in the butter and remove to a baking dish that later will be used for serving. Blend and brown the flour in the butter remaining in the pan. Stir in the salt, catsup, jelly, vinegar, bay leaf, water, and the remaining rum. Pour this, along with half the mushrooms, over the meat. Cover and bake at 350° for 1½ hours. Now arrange the rest of the mushrooms over the meat, re-cover, and allow to bake another 20 to 30 minutes. Serve with a mound of parsley piled in the center of the dish, and a big bowl of steamed rice or mashed potatoes on the side.

Lamb

An awesome spectacle to the Poor Poet is the sign, "Leg of Lamb—SPECIAL". Shall he splurge—roast the whole thing—invite all hungry friends—have a true feast? Or shall he turn away from this temptation, which could likewise turn out to be an extravagant gesture?

The best alternative is advanced practice with home butchering, although a leg of lamb is a bit more tricky than attacking a chuck or veal roast.

Although it requires a small saw, the easiest method is to slice several steaks from the sirloin end, leaving the balance for a roast.

Somewhat more involved, for only a boning knife is used, is to cut into the meat along the pelvic bone until the ball and socket bone are reached. The leg is then cut from the opposite side straight to the socket-bone cut. This results in a solid piece of meat for stew or curry, bones for soup, and the remainder of the leg for a roast. For Poor Poets who find the sight of the round socket bone protruding slightly from the roast unaesthetic, use of a saw or individual décor is recommended.

LAMB ROAST   ↻ 4–6
WITH POTATOES AND ONIONS

A true Sunday-dinner-type roast in which (Eureka!) the gravy is not made at the last minute. Vegetables cook with the roast, and there is nothing left to do but toss the salad and uncork the wine.

leg of lamb	*2 onions*
fresh beef fat or suet	*2 tablespoons chopped*
salt and pepper	*parsley*
6 *or* 8 *potatoes*	1 *tablespoon butter*

Rub the lamb with beef drippings and salt, and roast for one hour in a 400° oven, turning it to brown well all over. Remove the meat from the pan. Make gravy, and set it aside. Peel and slice the vegetables and lay them in the roasting pan. Sprinkle with parsley, butter, pepper, and a little salt. Add enough boiling water to barely cover and bring to a boil. Place the leg of lamb on the vegetables and return the pan to the oven. Continue roasting for an additional hour. Reheat the gravy just before serving.

GROUNDNUT CHOP   ♋ 4–6

If any of the roast is left over the following technique is recommended.

2 *pounds diced cooked lamb*   ⅔ *cup crunchy peanut*
2 *tablespoons olive oil*   *butter*
2¾ *cups water*   ¼ *teaspoon nutmeg*
1 *teaspoon paprika*   *salt and pepper*

Mix all the ingredients and simmer for 15 minutes. Serve over rice with side dishes of chutney and coconut.

CURRIED LAMB   ♋ 4
WITH WHITE WINE

2 *pounds lamb cut for stew or 4 lamb shanks*
4 *tablespoons oil*
4 *tablespoons flour*
1½ *teaspoons curry powder*
1 *cup water*
1 *cup dry white wine*
1 *onion, thinly sliced*
   salt, garlic salt, and pepper

Heat oil in a heavy skillet with a good lid. Brown the lamb slowly but well and remove. Add flour and curry powder to the drippings and blend well; add water and wine and cook and stir until thickened. Season. Return the lamb to the pan along with the onions. Cover and simmer for 1½ hours, or until meat is tender. Serve with rice.

Pork

Pork roasts usually come with the bones cut part way through, so little effort is required to remove several chops and thus reduce the size of the initial roast. Reserve the roast for a special occasion and start, in true Poor Poet style, with this homesy-folksy dish.

WINTER SQUASH AND PORK

Merely overlap slices of squash and pork shoulder. Sprinkle with brown sugar, butter, a little liquid gravy coloring and, perhaps, a grating of orange rind. Cover and bake for 40 minutes at 350°. Uncover and continue to bake until the meat is brown and tender.

GOLDEN GATE PORK ♄ 4

1 *pound lean pork*
  shoulder
1 *cup bouillon*
2 *green peppers*
1 *large onion*
4 *slices canned pineapple*
¼ *teaspoon ginger*

3 *tablespoons cornstarch*
¼ *cup sugar*
¼ *cup cider vinegar*
  soy sauce
  pepper
½ *cup pineapple syrup*

In a little fat trimmed from the pork, brown meat which has been cut in 1-inch cubes. Season with pepper, ginger, and a dash of soy sauce and add bouillon. Cover and simmer gently for 20 minutes. Cut the peppers into chunks and peel and dice the onion. Add these, along with pineapple cut into pieces, and cook no longer than 5 minutes. Blend the cornstarch and sugar with vinegar, a teaspoon of soy sauce, and the syrup. Add to above and stir until thickened. This will take 3 to 5 minutes. Serve over steamed rice.

SUNDAY LOIN OF PORK
WITH LIMAS

1 *pound dry lima beans*
4 *teaspoons salt*
4 *pounds loin of pork*
2 *large onions*
2 *bay leaves*
¼ *cup brown sugar*
¼ *teaspoon pepper*

Cover the limas with water and soak overnight. (A sprinkling of unseasoned meat tenderizer will speed up the forthcoming cooking time.) Drain, cover with fresh water and 2 teaspoons salt, and cook over low heat for about an hour.

In the meantime, salt and roast the pork in a 325° oven for 1 hour (30 minutes per pound). When the meat is half done, spoon drained beans around the roast along with ½ cup of the bean liquid, onions peeled and cut in wedges, and other ingredients. Continue roasting until the meat is done, checking every so often that there is a bit of liquid in the bottom of the pan.

ROAST PORK, TROPICAL STYLE

ↄ 6

4 *pounds loin of pork*
  soy sauce, garlic, ginger, salt, and pepper
6 *bananas*

Rub the seasonings well into the pork, and let stand for about an hour. Roast in a 325° oven at 30 minutes per pound. About a half hour before serving time peel the bananas and cut in half cross-wise. Lay them around the roast where they will cook in the drippings to a golden brown.

PORK SATE

An exciting combination that was initially whipped up as a marinade for bits of pork that would be roasted over charcoal. Then it was used on spareribs with great success. Finally, a loin of pork was rubbed and soaked in the same mixture, then roasted in the oven, with excellent results. Ingredients listed are sufficient for 1½ pounds of pork.

4 tablespoons peanut butter
2 tablespoons ground
  coriander
1 teaspoon salt
1 teaspoon black pepper
2 or 3 onions

2 cloves garlic
1 teaspoon lemon juice
2 tablespoons brown sugar
4 tablespoons soy sauce
1 chili pepper, seeded
2 or 3 tablespoons salad oil

Chop the onions and garlic and then mash all the ingredients to a paste, using a mortar, chopping bowl, or (what luck) electric blender.

Veal

May, splendid in new green grass and flowers, is calf time in the cattle country. This means Poor Poet-priced veal in abundance in all the markets.

1 4- to 5-pound rump roast will make a boneless roast for six with enough slices for a completely different dinner, PLUS a small bone for soup. Merely cut the necessary number of slices from the full end of the rump. (These may later be pounded quite thin.) This will expose the hipbone, which is easy to cut around and remove.

VEAL ROAST WITH PAPRIKA   ひ 6–8

3- to 4-*pound boned veal rump*
1 *large onion*
½ *teaspoon salt*
2 *teaspoons paprika*
⅛ *teaspoon pepper*
½ *pound fat salt pork*

Peel and chop the onion and stuff it into the cavity from the blade bone. Fold meat over, and tie with string. Rub salt, paprika, and pepper well into the roast. Now slice the salt pork and lay the strips over the roast. They should be fastened down with toothpicks. Roast the veal in a slow oven (325°) at 30 minutes per pound.

This roast is excellent served with noodles that have been tossed with a handful of chopped parsley. A squeeze of lemon juice or a grating of lemon rind added to the veal gravy is interesting. Brandy is fascinating.

VEAL ROAST,   ひ 6–8
HAPPY HUNGARIAN

3- to 4-*pound boned veal rump roast*
½ *pound fat salt pork*
½ *cup flour*
1 *teaspoon salt*
1½ *pints sour cream*
⅛ *teaspoon pepper*
2 *teaspoons paprika*
1 *jigger brandy*
3 *tablespoons minced onion*

Slice the salt pork and lay it over the bottom of a roasting pan with a cover. Rub flour and salt into the veal roast, and lay it on the salt pork bed. Mix the remaining ingredients and pour over the meat. Cover and roast 2½ hours at 350°. Turn the meat quite often and baste with the pan gravy. About 15 minutes before serving remove the cover so that the meat will brown on top. Mashed potatoes or noodles go with this roast.

3½ *pounds veal stew meat*
2 *cloves garlic*
⅛ *pound butter*
1 *heaping tablespoon*
 tomato preserves or
 currant jelly

2 *tablespoons dry vermouth*
1 *cup dry white wine*
2 *big tablespoons parsley*
1 *cup chicken stock*
½ *pound mushrooms*

Freeze the meat and then cut in thin slices. Dry well and brown in butter. Place the meat in a baking dish. Brown garlic slivers in the butter and reserve them. Brown the flour slightly and then add preserves, wines, and stock. Blend and thicken. Now add parsley, garlic, and sliced mushrooms. Pour this sauce over the veal, cover, and bake an hour or so at 375°.

VEAL ROSEMARY ⟨ 4

2 *pounds veal stew meat*
1 *cup white port*
¾ *cup cream*
5 *tablespoons butter*
2 *cloves garlic*
1 *teaspoon crushed rosemary*
½ *pound mushrooms*
 salt, pepper, and flour

Freeze, slice, and dry the veal. Slice mushrooms and brown in butter. Reserve. Simmer garlic in butter and discard the cloves. Now back to the meat. Flour it, and brown well. Then add the wine, cover, and simmer 1 hour. Then it is time to stir in the mushrooms, rosemary, and cream. Season with salt and a little pepper. Taste to see how everything is progressing, and allow the dish to cook for 10 minutes longer. Veal Rosemary definitely requires buttered noodles.

VEAL VERONICA   ❧ 4

A nice solution for people who, like Veronica, maintain kitchens the size of hall closets.

4 *thin veal steaks*
1 *tablespoon butter*
1 *can condensed cream of mushroom soup*
½ *cup dry white wine*

Pound the steaks into thin, uniform pieces, and brown in butter. Combine soup and wine and spoon over the steaks. Cover and simmer gently for 45 minutes. Instant mashed potatoes, a jar of pickled peaches, and a salad are workable accompaniments for the miniscule kitchen.

VEAL WITH MUSHROOMS   ❧ 4

A rich dish!

2 *pounds veal, thinly sliced*
  butter
½ *pound mushrooms*
1 *cup heavy cream*
1 *jigger brandy*
  salt and pepper
  flour
1 *cup water*

Roll veal in flour and brown in butter, then remove meat. Pour one cup of water into the remaining butter and veal juices and simmer this sauce to reduce it. Slice mushrooms, put them in a second pan with a lump of butter, and toss for about 5 minutes over medium heat. The mushrooms now go over the meat. And over both go the sauce and the cream, along with a little salt and pepper. Cover and place in a 375° oven for 20 minutes. Add the brandy just before serving.

Ground Beef

Ground beef was invented for Poor Poets. Especially the least expensive regular grind when funds are short. When they are not, he can graduate to ground chuck; splurge on ground round.

Then, when funds are holding their own, there is the coarse single grind to consider. Use of the latter, often packaged in supermarkets as "ground beef for chili", results in extra juicy, tender hamburger steaks. Because this grind is not at all compact, it makes meat loaves and meat balls that fall apart. Beware.

Ground beef delights Poor Poets because it can be used in divers ways. It is inadvisable but, with some imagination, a complete ground beef dinner could be devised. It might start with appetizers of cocktail-size meat balls to be dipped in cheese sauce. Following that would be bowls of minestrone-hamburger soup. And then might come spaghetti, or lasagna, or even stuffed peppers or cabbage rolls. The whole could always be topped off by a mincemeat some-thing-or-other. But this last might tip the scale too far, and the poet would forever lose his taste for ground beef. A sad situation indeed.

Because many of the One Pots with Meat rely heavily on ground beef, let us here consider only three or four things. First is:

A HAMBURGER SANDWICH

This hamburger sandwich is not one encased in bread or a roll. It is a filling sandwiched between two thin patties of hamburger. It is served on a plate. Only if the latter is missing, or if one is going walking, is a bread covering allowed.

Figure on one pound of hamburger for every four persons. For each serving pat the meat into two equal-size discs. Pile whatever filling desired on one disc. Top it with the other, seal the edges, and broil the meat.

Or—

If the hamburgers are sautéed in a skillet, a further step can be taken. As soon as the meat is removed, splash a little red wine, brandy, bourbon, or rum into the pan. (If the pan is very hot this maneuver will cause great spitting and possibly some blue flames.) Stir the sauce for perhaps a minute and pour it over the meat.

Hamburger sauce-making has a dual purpose. Flavor, of course. Furthermore, it tends to remove a lot of the meat particles stuck in the pan—contributing to easier dish washing.

Now, to the stuffing possibilities.

Chopped green onions with their tops
Chopped garlic
Chopped parsley and/or celery leaves
Chopped green or ripe olives
Chopped bell pepper
Crumbled blue cheese (or any cheese)
Toasted sesame seeds
Coarsely ground peanuts
LOTS *of paprika*
Chopped capers
Drained crushed pineapple
Applesauce
½ teaspoon curry powder moistened with ½ jigger brandy

A LARGE MEAT BALL ❧ 4

This is a make-in-the-cool-of-the-morning-and-eat-at-the-end-of-a-hot-day dish. It also has a by-product: soup stock.

1½ *pounds ground beef*
4 *slices bread*
1 *egg*
2 *tablespoons Parmesan cheese*
1 *heaping teaspoon chopped parsley*
1 *teaspoon crushed basil*
¼ *teaspoon salt*

2 *quarts water*
1 *stalk celery with leaves*
1 *large onion*
1 *large carrot*
1 *tomato or a big tablespoon of tomato paste*
2 *stalks parsley*
dash of salt

Soak the bread in some water or wine, squeeze dry, and crumble into the meat. Now add the egg, cheese, parsley, basil, and salt; mix well and form into one large meat ball. Shroud the meat ball in cheesecloth and immerse it in the boiling soup stock that's been made from the remaining ingredients. Lower the heat and simmer for 2 hours.

Remove the meat to a plate, discard the cheesecloth, and let the meat ball drain and cool. Tuck it in the refrigerator until ready to serve cold with a caper sauce:

2 *tablespoons capers*
6 *anchovy fillets*
  olive oil
  juice of one lemon
  cracked pepper

Pound the capers and anchovies in a mortar, adding olive oil little by little until there is about a cup of sauce. Finish with the lemon juice and pepper. But no salt; the anchovies take care of that. This sauce is also excellent with fish.

KID STUFF ♄ 4

This is on the sweet side, so very appropriate for children. Adults like it, too.

1 *pound ground beef*	$\frac{1}{8}$ *teaspoon pepper*
1 *small onion*	$\frac{1}{2}$ *cup chili sauce*
1 *teaspoon chili powder*	4 *strips bacon*
1 *teaspoon salt*	4 *canned apricot halves*

Chop the onion and combine gently with ground beef, chili powder, salt, pepper, and chili sauce. Form into four patties, wrap a wall of bacon around each, and fasten with a toothpick. Top each with an apricot half. Now bake in a hot, 450° oven for 20 to 25 minutes.

HAMBURGER, ♄ 6
RED FLANNEL STYLE

1$\frac{1}{2}$ *pounds ground beef*	1 *medium onion*
1 *cup mashed potatoes*	2 *tablespoons capers*
1 *egg*	1 *teaspoon salt*
$\frac{1}{2}$ *cup evaporated milk*	$\frac{1}{2}$ *teaspoon pepper*
$\frac{1}{2}$ *cup chopped pickled beets*	*chopped parsley*

Chop the onions and capers with the pickled beets. Combine everything but the parsley and mix thoroughly. Now pat out twelve little steaks or six big ones. Sauté these in butter and sprinkle with parsley just before serving. Some sort of pickled fruit goes nicely on the side.

Variety Meats

The Poor Poet of the Orient dries and pulverizes the variety meats, sprinkling them over assorted dishes for an energy boost. His colleague directly across the Pacific buys the same meats canned or fresh, feeding them to his sleek cat and purchasing vitamins regularly.

This brief section is therefore designed for the squeamish ("I'd *never* touch—") as an introduction to an interesting assortment of viands.

HEART

Veal hearts, which weigh about a pound each (one will serve two people), are the best choice. Beef hearts, which are three or four times larger, are less expensive, though tougher. They can be bought sliced, and after cutting away the veins and hard parts, should be soaked overnight in buttermilk or water and lemon juice. After cooking, beef hearts should be served immediately, for they will toughen if allowed to stand.

Whole beef hearts can be stuffed, tied, and cooked as a pot roast. Ground beef heart can be mixed with pork sausage, seasoned with garlic, thyme, nutmeg, marjoram, and sage and otherwise prepared as a meat loaf.

Sliced beef heart makes a fine steak.

BEEF HEART STEAKS   ↺ 4

2 *pounds beef heart*   1 *large clove garlic*
  olive oil   *juice of one lemon*
  salt and pepper   *chopped parsley*

Tenderize the heart as noted above, or use a meat tenderizer. Dry the meat, slice thin and marinate in ¼ cup olive oil, ½ teaspoon salt, and ¼ teaspoon pepper for at least 30 minutes.

Sauté one clove of garlic in 3 or 4 tablespoons of olive oil and discard. Now add the heart and brown it well on both sides over high heat. Continue to cook for 8 minutes, turning the slices frequently. Serve sprinkled with salt, pepper, lemon juice, and chopped parsley.

LIVER

Lamb liver is too dry; calves liver is too dear. Pork liver is the best buy, with that from beef running a close second.

LIVER WITH LEMON AND PARSLEY ℃ 2

1 *pound pork liver*
juice of one lemon
2 *heaping tablespoons chopped parsley*
salt and pepper

Marinate the liver in lemon and parsley for about an hour. Sauté in butter and serve sprinkled with additional parsley, salt, and pepper. Good with mashed potatoes, and a good gravy can be made from the fat and scraps in the pan.

NANKING LIVER ℃ 3–4

1 *pound pork liver*	1 *tablespoon cornstarch*
2 *tablespoons soy sauce*	6 *tablespoons oil*
1 *tablespoon sherry*	2 *bunches green onions*
¼ *teaspoon sugar*	¼ *teaspoon pepper*

Cut the liver in narrow strips and let soak in soy sauce, sherry, sugar, and cornstarch for 10 minutes or longer. In the meantime thinly slice the green onions.

Bring the oil to a bubble in a heavy frying pan. Toss in the slightly drained liver and cook for 3 minutes, stirring constantly with a fork or chopsticks. Mix in the green onions and cook an additional 2 or 3 minutes. Sprinkle with pepper. Steamed rice accompanies this, and more soy sauce on the side.

LIVER PÂTÉ

Because grinding liver is not the most glorious of tasks, because an oven going for 4 hours uses a considerable amount of fuel, and because this pâté keeps so well, it is advisable to concoct this in gargantuan portions. So this formula should fill a 4-quart mold or the equivalent in little molds.

4 *pounds pork liver*	¼ *cup brandy*
4 *pounds bacon*	½ *cup white wine*
2 *or 3 cloves garlic*	½ *cup water*
1 *medium onion*	2 *carrots*
¼ *teaspoon mace*	2 *onions*
¼ *teaspoon ground cloves*	*rosemary, thyme, and*
¼ *teaspoon pepper*	*bay leaf*

Grind the liver, bacon, garlic, and onion. If the liver is first frozen and then cut into finger-size pieces, it is far easier to grind. Mix the spices with the ground meat and pour the mixture into a well-greased straight-sided baking dish with a cover. Top the pâté with the brandy, wine, and water, sliced carrots, and onions, and the herbs. Cover and place in a larger pan of water. A roasting pan does nicely. Cover and bake at 275° to 300° for 3 or 4 hours.

Remove the vegetables and cool the pâté. Seal it with pork lard and refrigerate. Some of the pâté may be wrapped and frozen, although its texture will not be so smooth.

OXTAILS

Economical and rich in flavor and protein is the whip-like oxtail, revered in mythology for its strength and wisdom. Disjointed, not hacked up aimlessly with a cleaver, and well browned, the pieces make superb soups or stews.

OXTAILS VERMOUTH ♋ 6

4½ pounds disjointed oxtails	1 teaspoon salt
1 or 2 tablespoons	½ teaspoon pepper
shortening	1 cup dry vermouth
½ cup chopped celery	4 cups water
¾ cup chopped onions	1½ cups sliced mushrooms
1 large clove garlic	½ cup sliced stuffed green
⅛ teaspoon rosemary	olives
⅛ teaspoon thyme	2 tablespoons cornstarch

Brown oxtails in a heavy pan and then brown the vegetables. Add the herbs, salt, pepper, vermouth, and water. Cover tightly and simmer in a 325° oven for 2 to 2½ hours. Now toss in the mushrooms and olives and continue cooking for another half hour. Skim excess fat and thicken with cornstarch mixed with a little water.

This is a rich dish, and anything left over seems even better the next day.

SAUSAGES

Larger markets abound with all sorts of sausages and although the next two recipes were designed for pork links, experimentation with other varieties is requested.

SAUSAGES IN BEER

1½ *pounds link sausages*
1 *large onion*
1 *tablespoon bacon fat*
2 *cups beer*
1 *bay leaf*
3 *peppercorns*
2 *tablespoons flour*
   salt

Brown the sausages and chopped onion in bacon fat. Add 1 cup beer, the bay leaf and peppercorns, bring to a boil, and allow the beer to reduce by half. Sprinkle with a little salt and add the rest of the beer. Cover and simmer for 20 minutes. Remove the sausages and discard the peppercorns. Thicken the sauce and serve it over the sausages and with plenty of mashed potatoes. Cole slaw is good with this, and perhaps some applesauce.

SAUSAGES IN WHITE WINE

1½ *pounds pork sausages*
1 *cup consommé*
1½ *cups dry white wine*
1 *stalk celery*
1 *large carrot*
   chopped parsley or green onion tops

Parboil the sausages and drain. Chop the vegetables as fine as possible. Combine all ingredients except the parsley and simmer for 15 to 20 minutes. If desired, thicken the sauce with a little flour. Serve with mashed potatoes, and use a lavish sprinkling of parsley to avoid an anemic dish. Furthermore, never serve Sausages in White Wine on white plates.

POINDEXTER SCRAPPLE   ↺ 4–6

1 *cup hominy grits*
1 *pound bulk pork sausage*
3 *large eggs*

Cook the grits as directed on the package and, in the meantime, fry and crumble the sausage. Drain it well and beat into the cooked grits along with the three eggs. Pour into a buttered mold and chill. Slice the scrapple and brown in lots of butter. Serve awash with maple syrup.

BAJA CALIFORNIA SCRAPPLE   ↺ 4–6

½ *pound bacon or salt pork*
2 *large onions*
1 *large clove garlic*
1¼ *cups cornmeal*
½ *teaspoon chili powder*
¼ *teaspoon oregano*
¼ *teaspoon cumin*
¼ *cup sliced stuffed green olives*

Dice the bacon, onions, and garlic, brown well and reserve. Cook the cornmeal and spices in a double boiler, following directions on cornmeal package. In about 45 minutes, at which time the cornmeal should be done, add the browned bacon-onions and the olives. Stir well, pour into a greased, 1-quart mold, and chill. The scrapple is now ready to slice and fry. It goes fine with eggs or applesauce.

4 *pounds corned beef*
4 *tablespoons liquid smoke sauce*
4 *large cloves garlic*
1 *enormous onion*
2 *tablespoons pickling spices*
6 *to* 8 *tablespoons coarsely ground pepper*

Rub the corned beef with 2 tablespoons liquid smoke sauce, wrap closely in foil, and refrigerate overnight. The next day unwrap the meat and simmer it, along with the garlic, onion, pickling spices, and the remaining 2 tablespoons liquid smoke sauce, in water to cover for 2½ hours. (It is not necessary to peel the garlic, although the onion should be peeled and cut in large hunks.) Cool the meat in the broth, then remove, pat dry with paper towels, and rub pepper all over the surface, building up a layer thick enough that little meat shows through. Encase the pastrami in aluminum foil and store in the refrigerator for at least 2 days. Slice *very* thin to serve.

Chicken

In the thirties poultry producers happened upon the battery-raising method used by the early Romans, improved upon it, and ever since the possibility of "a chicken in every pot" has been a reality.

Not only that, but the experts tell us that chicken is low in calories, high in protein, and pound for pound always an excellent buy.

So the problem posed the Poor Poet is not "Shall we have chicken?" but "*How* shall we have it?"

1 *whole frying chicken*   *salt*
2 *or* 3 *large cloves garlic*   *freshly cracked pepper*
   juice of 2 *lemons*

Place the chicken on a roasting pan, slide it into the oven, and roast at 325° until the chicken is tender (45 minutes to an hour). In the meantime, mash the garlic in a mortar and then mix in the lemon juice, a scant teaspoon salt, and at least a half teaspoon cracked pepper.

When the chicken is done, cut it up on a serving platter and pour over it the garlic-lemon sauce along with any juice from the pan. This is good with rice, or with crisp rolls that can be dunked into the juice.

OVEN-BROILED CHICKEN

Frying chicken or broilers, split, washed, dried and variously seasoned, are broiled—skin side down—in a hot (450°) oven for about 45 minutes. The halves are juicy on the inside and have exceptionally crisp skin. Figure roughly on half a 2-pound chicken per person.

HERB-SMOTHERED CHICKEN

Rub chicken halves with a generous amount of oil or butter and mashed garlic. Sprinkle liberally with salt, pepper, paprika, rosemary, basil, or oregano. Broil as above, basting two or three times with the fat in the pan, and a splash of sherry or dry vermouth.

CHICKEN D'ORO ℃ 2

1 *split frying chicken*
1 *large orange*
2 *teaspoons paprika*
1 *teaspoon salt*
¼ *teaspoon pepper*
½ *stick butter*

Melt the butter in the roasting pan and rub some over the chicken halves. Then pat each half with grated orange rind, paprika, salt, and pepper. Broil as above, basting two or three times with the fat in the pan and juice from the orange.

PHOENIX ℃ 2

1 *split frying chicken*
  rosemary, basil, garlic, salt, and pepper
½ *stick butter*
¼ *cup light or golden rum*
  celery leaves or similar greenery
  paprika

Proceed as for Herb-Smothered Chicken. When ready to serve, bed the chicken on a platter of green leaves dusted with paprika. Heat the rum, ignite, and pour over the chicken.

CHICKEN WITH PARMESAN ℃ 2
AND YOGURT

1 *split frying chicken*
½ *cup yogurt*
1 *clove garlic*
4 *tablespoons Parmesan cheese*
  salt and pepper
½ *stick butter*

Rub the chicken halves with yogurt and mashed garlic and allow to stand for several hours. Now dust the halves with salt, pepper, and grated Parmesan. Place, skin side down, in a generously buttered pan, and broil as above, basting several times with the fat in the pan or with additional butter.

Because yogurt acts as a tenderizer, this is a wise method to follow when one is in doubt as to the age of the chicken.

FRIED CHICKEN

CHICKEN, AQUARIUM STYLE   ℃ 2–4

A lady visiting a nearby aquarium not long ago had her purse snapped up by an alligator. After 2 hours of contented chewing, while being tapped on the head with a long pole (this is said to make alligators spit), he forfeited the bag—contents intact except for a package of lemon drops.

This leads to contemplation of the value of pre-lemon flavored alligator meat, and because these creatures are said to taste like chicken, of the value of seasoning the latter with lemon or lime.

1 *chicken, cut for frying*
3 *large lemons or limes*
  salt and pepper
  butter or shortening

Dry the chicken pieces, sprinkle with salt and pepper, and fry in butter along with one thinly sliced lime. When nearly done, squeeze the juice of the second lime over the chicken. Serve with rice that is seasoned with soy sauce and the juice of the third lime.

1 3½–4-*pound chicken, cut for frying*
1 *egg*
½ *cup milk*
½ *cup flour*
½ *teaspoon baking powder*
2 *teaspoons paprika*
2 *teaspoons salt*
1 *teaspoon pepper*
¼ *cup* finely *chopped peanuts*
¼ *cup sesame seeds*
1 *stick butter or* ¼ *cup shortening*

Beat the egg and milk together. Dip chicken pieces into this and then into flour mixed with baking powder, salt, pepper, paprika, nuts, and sesame seeds. (Although shaking chicken and seasoned flour together in a paper bag is generally the best idea, it doesn't work well here, as the nuts and seeds tend to remain off the chicken and in the bag.)

Fry the chicken until it is nicely browned. Add a tablespoon or two of water and cover the pan loosely. Cook over low heat for about 45 minutes or until chicken is tender.

If gravy is called for, add 1½ cups milk to drippings in pan and heat to scalding. Mix 4 tablespoons flour with an additional ½ cup milk, add to the pan and cook, stirring constantly until the gravy is thick and smooth. Season with salt, pepper, lots of paprika, and a good dash of sherry.

CHICKEN IN A POT

CHICKEN FRICASSÉE   ✌ 4–5

1 4–5-*pound stewing hen*	½ *bay leaf*
2 *cups water*	*dash of thyme*
2 *cups dry white wine*	6 *crushed juniper berries*
1½ *teaspoons salt*	*or* ¼ *cup gin*
1 *large carrot*	3 *tablespoons flour*
1 *large onion*	½ *cup thin cream*
3 *or* 4 *sprigs parsley and*	2 *egg yolks*
celery tops	1 *cup hot cooked peas*

Bring water, 1 cup wine, salt, cut-up vegetables, the juniper berries or gin, and herbs to a boil. Plunk in the chicken, cover, and simmer until tender. This will take about 2 hours, but cooking time can be considerably cut if frying chickens are substituted for stewing hens.

When the chicken is done, remove it and keep hot. Discard the vegetables and skim excess fat. Pour in the remaining cup of wine, reheat, and thicken with flour mixed with cream and egg yolks. Return the chicken to the pot, along with the peas, and let the fricassée heat well throughout. Great with mashed potatoes.

FRICASSÉE WITH BRANDY   ✌ 4

1 4–5-*pound stewing hen*	2 *ounces brandy*
½ *stick butter*	1 *cup cream*
1 *green onion with top*	2 *egg yolks*
1 *clove garlic*	*salt and pepper to taste*
½ *cup* each *dry red and*	
dry white wine	

Brown the chicken in butter along with the cut-up onion and garlic. Add the wine, salt and pepper, and when the mixture boils add and flame the brandy. Cover the pan, reduce heat, and simmer until the chicken is tender. If the liquid gets too low, replenish it with water or more wine.

Place the chicken on a serving dish, and thicken the liquid remaining in the pan with egg yolks beaten with cream. Stir briskly and see that the sauce is not allowed to boil.

Serve the chicken with the sauce poured over and a dish of steamed rice on the side. A handful of sliced mushrooms (preferably fresh, but drained if canned), tossed in when the chicken is half done, is not to be frowned upon.

CHICKEN EDGEWOOD   ଓ 4–6

2 *frying chickens,*
    2–2½-pounds
½ *cup flour*
2 *teaspoons salt*
1 *teaspoon garlic powder*
1 *teaspoon pepper*
½ *cup shortening*

2 *bananas*
1 *pound yams, parboiled*
2 *large oranges*
4 *or 5 chili teppins*
½ *teaspoon nutmeg*
½ *cup chopped parsley*

Shake cut-up chicken, flour, garlic powder, salt, and pepper together in a paper bag. Brown the chicken well in hot shortening, add 2 or 3 tablespoons of water, cover the skillet loosely and cook over low heat for 30 minutes.

Quarter the bananas and unpeeled oranges, and cut the yams in thick slabs. Seed and crush the chillies. Add all these, along with nutmeg, to the chicken. Re-cover and continue cooking until the chicken is done, about 15 minutes. Serve strewn with parsley. Rice is the preferred side dish.

LEFTOVER CHICKEN

Well, there's always creamed chicken (or turkey) but here are two with a difference.

CORAL CHICKEN   ℃ 6

½ *small onion, minced*
¼ *cup butter*
1 *cup sliced mushrooms (preferably fresh, but drained if canned)*
1 *teaspoon paprika*
1 *teaspoon salt*
¼ *teaspoon nutmeg*
6 *slices cooked chicken white meat*
6 *slices cooked ham*
1½ *cups rich milk (or 1 cup milk and ½ cup chicken stock)*
¼ *cup dry white wine or light sherry*
4 *tablespoons grated Parmesan cheese*

Melt the butter in a baking dish and sauté the onion until it is tender. Add mushrooms and seasonings and cook for 5 minutes. Lay the slices of chicken and ham on the mushroom bed and nearly drown with milk and wine.

Bake in a 400° oven for 10 minutes, sprinkle with grated cheese, and return to the oven to brown.

AMIGO   ℃ 4–6

So named because more of any of the three main ingredients may be added without noticeably affecting the taste but noticeably increasing the number of servings.

1 *one-pound jar tamales*
1 *to 2 cups shredded cooked chicken or turkey*
1 *8-ounce can tomato sauce*
1 *one-pound can whole-kernel corn*
1 *4-ounce can chopped olives*
¼ *cup raisins*
2 *teaspoons chili powder*
¾ *cup chicken stock*
  dash of sherry
  salt and pepper to taste
¾ *cup grated Parmesan or Cheddar cheese*

Lay the tamales in a buttered baking dish and cover with shredded chicken. Mix the other ingredients, except for cheese, taste for seasoning, and pour over the tamales and chicken. Sprinkle with cheese and bake at 350° for 45 minutes to an hour.

WINGS, BACKBONES, AND GIBLETS AS CHOICE ITEMS

Smiling bravely, someone will claim, "But I *like* backbones"—or wingtips, necks, gizzards. Paltry fare, at best, if consumed in lieu of a fat drumstick. However, given individual treatment, the less choice parts become very choice indeed.

Congee, the thick rice soup (page 15), is one cold-weather answer. Spaghetti sauce made from giblets instead of ground beef is another. Then there are dishes calling for a fair quantity of a specific part; ingredients are come by either through patience and freezer-storage or a visit to a poultry market.

2 *pounds chicken wings*
⅓ *cup soy sauce*
¾ *cup dry sherry*
2 *teaspoons grated ginger or* 1 *teaspoon powdered ginger*
1 *large clove garlic*

———

1 *egg*
⅔ *cup water*
1 *cup flour*
  oil for frying

Simmer chicken wings in water until they are tender. Reserve the stock for soup and marinate the wings in the combined soy sauce, sherry, ginger, and mashed garlic for several hours. Drain. Reserve marinade.

Beat the egg with ⅓ cup of the soy-sherry marinade, water, and flour. Dip wings in flour, then in the batter. Fry in deepish fat (300–350°) until puffy and golden.

CHICKEN GIBLETS AND VERMICELLI   ও 4

1 *pound chicken giblets*
2 *tablespoons olive oil*
2 *large onions*
2 *or* 3 *large tomatoes*
1 *teaspoon salt*
¼ *teaspoon pepper*

1 *teaspoon paprika*
¼ *teaspoon each thyme and marjoram*
½ *cup water*
¾ *pound vermicelli*

Chop giblets slightly and, reserving the livers, brown along with chopped onions in olive oil. Add the coarsely chopped tomatoes, seasonings, and water. Cover and simmer about an hour or until the giblets are tender. Add the livers about 10 minutes before the giblets are done.

In the meantime, toast vermicelli in the oven until it is a light golden color. Boil in salted water until soft, drain, and combine with the sauce. Simmer to heat through.

A green salad with olive oil, red wine, and crusty bread accompany this dish.

CHICKEN LIVERS, SWEET AND PUNGENT
ʊ 4

1 *pound chicken livers*
2 *tablespoons oil*
1 *cup chicken bouillon*
4 *slices canned pineapple*
3 *large green peppers, seeds removed*

3 *tablespoons cornstarch*
2 *teaspoons soy sauce*
½ *cup cider vinegar*
½ *cup sugar*
  salt and pepper

Cut the livers in two pieces each and cook quickly in hot fat, with a little salt and pepper, until light brown. Remove and keep warm. Add ⅓ cup bouillon, cut-up pineapple and peppers, cover and simmer 5 minutes.

Mix the cornstarch, soy sauce, vinegar, sugar, and ⅔ cup bouillon. Add to the other ingredients and cook and stir for 5 minutes, or until the sauce is thick and clear. Pour sauce over the livers and serve with rice.

RUMAKI
ʊ 2–4

Rumaki take care and patience to make. They are meant for someone who is loved.

1 *pound chicken livers*
1 *can water chestnuts*
½ *pound thin-sliced bacon*

⅓ *cup sherry*
3 *tablespoons soy sauce*
  bamboo skewers

Cut each liver in two pieces and dip in boiling water so they are easier to work with. Cook the bacon until it is just limp and drain. Drain and slice the water chestnuts. Get out the skewers, and it is time to begin. Place a chestnut slice on each side of a piece of liver, wrap with bacon, and skewer. When all the Rumaki are so made, place them in a dish and drench with soy sauce and sherry. Let them soak for several hours, turning them occasionally.

Broil them over charcoal or in a 500° oven for 5 minutes. Serve them as hors d'œuvres or as an entrée with steamed rice.

BREADS

Third grade was a pinecone turkey at Thanksgiving and red and green paper chains at Christmas. It was percussion band and flash card and planting a tree each Arbor Day.

It was a sand table with little toy trucks and houses and a field in which real wheat grew.

It was Columbus and Magellan; but the only thing that remains distinct (and in the lower right page of the history book) is the picture of the last boy of Pompeii and his faithful dog. And next to the picture was a description of the boy's house and how the dishes were found, so much later, still on the table, along with a loaf of bread.

Today's bread doesn't keep quite that long, even with the addition of preservatives and fortifiers. Here are a few things to do with bread that's stood on the shelf many days—but not so many that it is shrouded in soft powdery blue mold. *

---

* Not to be overlooked are Poor Poet's Soufflé, Bread Pudding, croutons for soups and salads, and bread crumbs to feed to the birds in the park.

Glorifying Store Bread

ANISE TOAST

Lay thin slices of bread on a baking sheet. Sprinkle a little water over the slices and pat on a few anise seeds. Bake the bread at 300° until crisp and lightly browned.

PULLED BREAD

Use some care in pulling the insides from loaves used to make Breadloaves (page 137). Break the bread into serving-size pieces. Brush with melted butter and bake at 325° until crisp and brown. Pulled Bread can be used in place of rolls or crackers with salad or soup. The smaller pieces can be used for croutons.

MAPLE TOAST

Dip slices of bread in maple syrup and sauté in butter until light brown. Care must be taken so that the syrup candies but does not burn.

RUM TOAST

Make a syrup of brown sugar or honey and rum. Dip slices of bread in the syrup and proceed as for Maple Toast.

CANDIED JELLY TOAST

Melt tag ends of jelly in water or sherry and proceed as above.

CUSTARD TOAST ❧ 2–3

There are many French toasts, but this one is far superior.

> 6 *fairly thick slices of bread*
> 2 *eggs*
> 1 *cup rich milk*
> 1 *teaspoon sugar*
> ½ *teaspoon vanilla*
> ¼ *teaspoon nutmeg*
>   *lots of butter*

Beat together the eggs, milk, sugar, vanilla, and nutmeg. Dip slices of bread into the mixture, allowing each slice to soak in as much liquid as possible.

Sauté slowly in butter, turning once. The outside should be crisp while the inside is reminiscent of custard. Serve with syrup, jam, or a dusting of powdered sugar.

The addition of ¼ teaspoon baking powder to the liquid will make the toast even fluffier.

Pulled bread can be used for Custard Toast. In this case fry in hot deep fat (365°–375°).

BREAD AND WINE

> 1 *long loaf French bread*
> ⅓ *cup soft butter*
> ¼ *cup claret or Burgundy wine*
>   *dash of salt and cayenne*

Slash the loaf into thick slices, cutting almost to the bottom crust. Beat the wine, salt, and cayenne into the butter and spread between slices and over the top of the loaf.

Bake for 10 minutes at 400°. This is a welcome change from garlic bread, especially when garlic has been used with a lavish hand in accompanying dishes.

HERMIT GARLIC BREAD

The poet, or painter, or anyone who desires a few days' solitude is admonished to first dine on Hermit Bread. Red wine is good for washing down. The bread is also an excellent accompaniment to a thick soup and/or salad.

1 *long leaf French bread*
4 *tablespoons soft butter*
4 *large cloves garlic*
¼ *cup sherry*
1 *cup grated Parmesan cheese*

Slash the loaf, almost to the bottom crust. Mash the garlic and mix with the other ingredients. Spread the mixture between the slices, with a little saved for the top. Put the bread in a paper bag and sprinkle water over the bag. Bake 15 to 20 minutes at 350°. When the paper bag is crisp and beginning to brown the loaf is done.

OLIVE TILES

10 *slices day-old bread*
1 *cup chopped black olives*
1 *egg*
¼ *cup chopped onion*
2½ *cups grated Cheddar cheese*
    several dashes Tabasco
⅓ *cup olive oil or melted butter*

Beat the egg lightly and stir in the oil, onion, cheese, Tabasco, and olives. Lay the slices of bread on a lightly oiled baking pan and spread with the topping. Bake for 15 to 20 minutes at 400°.

Biscuits

Whether home-made, mix-made, or bought ready-to-bake, biscuits can be varied indefinitely in both design and flavor.

As to design, consider pinwheels, in which the dough is rolled on a board, spread with filling, rolled like a jelly roll, and finally sliced in sections about $\frac{3}{4}$ inch thick.

A twist can be fashioned in almost the same way, except that the roll is cut only about $\frac{2}{3}$ of the way through and each section is turned on its side, alternating to the right and left. (During which time a dry stuffing tends to come out.)

Thimbles are made with a small cutter; or thimbles and eights can be made with a doughnut cutter, the rings simply being twisted into figure eights.

Cats, dogs, men, turtles, and starfish, along with other inhabitants of the Ark or the deep, are not encouraged for everyday fare.

Packaged biscuit mixes are not to be frowned on. However, here's a good basic biscuit recipe for the make-it-from-scratch cook.

BASIC BISCUITS ✢ 1 dozen

2 *cups sifted all-purpose flour*
4 *teaspoons baking powder*
$\frac{1}{2}$ *teaspoon salt*
$\frac{1}{4}$ *cup shortening*
$\frac{3}{4}$ *cup milk*

Combine flour, baking powder, and salt in a mixing bowl. With a pastry blender, two knives, or finger tips, cut in the shortening until it is as fine as cornmeal. Add milk and stir gently with a fork until dough holds together. Turn the dough out into a lightly floured board, sprinkle a little flour over the top, and knead gently—about a dozen strokes. Pat the dough out until it is about $\frac{3}{4}$ inch thick. Cut with floured biscuit cutter, or go creative with the above designs, and place biscuits on a baking sheet about 1 inch apart. Bake at 450° for 12 to 15 minutes.

Here are some variations as to biscuit flavor. Amounts given are for a 2-cup flour batch of dough.

ONION BUNS: Sauté 1 cup thinly sliced onions in butter until golden. Mix half the onions in the dough and sprinkle the other half on top of the biscuits.

HERB BISCUITS: Add $\frac{1}{2}$ cup finely chopped parsley, green onions with tops, or chives, and $\frac{1}{2}$ teaspoon dry herbs (sage, marjoram, basil, savory, or thyme) to the dry ingredients. These make good tops or bases for meat pies or stewed chicken.

CHEESE BISCUITS: Add $\frac{1}{2}$ cup grated cheese to flour mixture.

SEED BISCUITS: Add 2 or 3 tablespoons poppy, anise, sesame, or caraway seeds to the flour mixture. Or dip biscuits in melted butter and then roll in seeds.

ORANGE BISCUITS: Add 1 tablespoon grated orange rind to the flour mixture and substitute orange juice for half the liquid.

COTTAGE CHEESE BISCUITS: Cut 1 cup of cottage cheese into the flour mixture and add just enough milk to make a soft dough.

PINEAPPLE BISCUITS: Substitute crushed pineapple and juice for the liquid. A grating of orange or lemon peel will pick up the flavor.

RAISIN BISCUITS: Add 1 cup of raisins, puffed in hot water and drained, to the dry ingredients. Or use half raisins and half broken walnuts.

1½ *cups biscuit dough*
2 *cups thinly sliced onions*
4 *tablespoons butter*
3 *eggs*
1½ *cups sour cream*
¼ *teaspoon salt*
  pepper
½ *teaspoon oregano or* 1 *tablespoon poppy seeds*

Pat the dough into a large greased pie pan and flute the edges so that the filling will not spill over. Add the onions that have been wilted in hot butter. Beat the eggs lightly and combine with the other ingredients. Pour this over the onions. Bake at 400° for 30 minutes or until the custard is set.

Scones and Quick Breads

SKILLET SCONES ❧ 2 dozen

These are excellent hot, with lots of butter, and not at all bad cold. Besides, they're one of the few breads that can be baked without an oven.

2 *cups sifted flour*   1 *large egg*
1 *tablespoon baking powder*   ¼ *cup salad oil*
2 *tablespoons sugar*   ¼ *cup cream or evaporated*
½ *teaspoon salt*   *milk*
½ *cup raisins or currants*

Mix and sift the dry ingredients and then toss in raisins. Beat egg and combine with oil and milk. Dump this all at once into the dry ingredients and mix lightly with a fork.

Turn dough onto a floured board and knead 5 to 10 minutes. Pat into two circles about ½ inch thick and cut each circle into twelve wedges. Bake on an ungreased griddle or heavy frying pan 6 to 10 minutes per side, or until scones are golden brown.

NON-CRUMBLING CORN CAKES ∾ 1 dozen

⅔ *cup cornmeal*
½ *cup unsifted flour*
2 *tablespoons sugar*
1 *teaspoon baking powder*
½ *teaspoon salt*

¼ *teaspoon baking soda*
½ *stick butter*
⅓ *cup milk*
1 *egg*

Sift dry ingredients together and cut in butter. Beat egg with the milk and pour into the cornmeal mixture, stirring only enough to moisten. Drop from a tablespoon onto a well-greased baking sheet. The cakes will spread to about 3 inches, so allot each one sufficient space. Bake at 375° for about 15 minutes.

BIB CORNBREAD

Unlike the preceding corn cakes, this bread tends to crumble down the shirtfront of the unwary. A nice excuse for using plenty of butter, maple syrup, or honey.

1 *cup yellow cornmeal*
1 *tablespoon sugar*
½ *teaspoon salt*
2 *tablespoons flour*
2 *tablespoons shortening*
1 *cup boiling water*
2 *large eggs*

Combine dry ingredients. Stir in the boiling water and shortening, mixing well and adding a little more water if it seems too dry. Set aside to cool, while separating the eggs and beating the yolks until lemony and the whites quite stiff. Now stir yolks into the cornmeal mixture, then fold in the whites. Pour into a well-greased 8-inch-square pan and bake 20 to 25 minutes at 400°.

IRISH SODA BREAD

To be eaten hot or cold, this is one quick bread that is good for sandwiches.

4 cups flour
2½ teaspoons salt
1 teaspoon baking soda
⅓ cup sugar
1 tablespoon caraway
  seeds

½ cup currants
½ cup raisins
2 cups buttermilk
1 egg

Combine all ingredients and work on a board with an additional ¾ cup flour. Shape into a round loaf, slash a cross on the top, place on a greased baking sheet, and bake for about 45 minutes at 350°. Thump the loaf on its bottom. If it sounds hollow, it's done.

Lazy Irish Bread can be made by adding a tablespoon each of shortening and sugar along with currants and caraway seeds to biscuit mix and milk. Then proceed as above.

IRISH BROWN BREAD

4⅓ cups sifted flour
3 teaspoons baking soda
1 teaspoon sugar
2 teaspoons salt
1⅔ cups crushed all-bran
2½ cups buttermilk

Sift dry ingredients and combine with crushed all-bran. Pour in buttermilk and stir just enough to moisten. Press dough into well-greased bread pan (9 × 5 × 3) and bake at 350° for 1 hour.

A handful of currants and a tablespoon of caraway seeds mixed with the dry ingredients is a pleasant variation. To some it is a necessity.

PUMPKIN BREAD

This is best cold with some butter or cream cheese.

2½ *cups sifted flour*	1 *cup chopped walnuts*
1 *tablespoon baking powder*	½ *cup shortening*
1 *teaspoon salt*	1 *cup brown sugar*
2 *teaspoons cinnamon*	2 *eggs*
1 *teaspoon ground cloves*	1 *cup buttermilk*
½ *teaspoon mace*	¾ *cup canned pumpkin*
½ *teaspoon baking soda*	

Sift together flour, baking powder, salt, spices, and soda. Mix in the walnuts. Cream shortening and sugar until light and fluffy, add eggs, and beat well. Combine buttermilk and pumpkin and add to the creamed mixture alternately with flour mixture. Turn batter into a well-greased 5½ × 9½-inch loaf pan. Bake at 350° for an hour and 15 minutes. Turn out of pan and cool on a rack.

V. I. P. COFFEE CAKE

This coffee cake is not frugal. It should be all eaten up while it is hot, for any remaining until the next day has the texture of a ponderous pound cake.

½ pound butter
1¼ cups sugar
2 eggs
1 cup sour cream
2 cups flour
½ teaspoon soda
1½ teaspoons baking
 powder
1 teaspoon vanilla

¾ cup finely chopped
 walnuts
1 teaspoon cinnamon
2 tablespoons sugar

Beat together the butter, sugar, and eggs until light and fluffy. Blend in the sour cream. Sift and measure flour and resift with dry ingredients. Add to the cream mixture and vanilla and blend gently but well.

Pour half the batter into a well-buttered and floured 9-inch tube pan. Sprinkle on half the walnut-cinnamon-sugar mixture. Pour in the remaining batter and top with remaining walnut mixture. Place in a cold oven, set to 350° and bake for 55 minutes. It will serve eight to ten.

Crackers

SCOTCH WHEAT THINS   ℭ 8 dozen

1½ cups graham flour
½ cup white flour
½ teaspoon salt
⅓ cup butter
1 tablespoon honey
⅓ cup boiling water

Cut butter into dry ingredients. Add honey and boiling water and mix well. (Throughout, hands work better than a fork or spoon.) Chill dough, roll *thin*, cut in squares or what have you, and bake 12 to 15 minutes at 325° or until crackers are crisp and light brown.

TAJ MAHAL FLATBREAD ♋ 2 dozen

This bread is necessary for a curry dinner, and also good with soup or salad.

1½ *cups flour*
1 *teaspoon turmeric*
¼ *teaspoon salt*
½ *teaspoon soda*
½ *teaspoon coarsely ground pepper*
½ *stick butter*
   water

Sift dry ingredients and blend in pepper and butter. Add only enough water to make a stiff dough. Pinch out marble-size balls and roll on a floured board to 4-inch rounds. Bake in an ungreased cookie sheet at 400° for 3 minutes. Turn with a spatula and bake on the other side for the same amount of time.

If an oven isn't available, the flatbread can be baked on a heavy griddle or skillet.

COWBOY BREAD ♋ 1 dozen

Not recommended for weight-watchers, Cowboy Bread is excellent with chili beans, highly seasoned stews, or big combination salads.

2 *cups flour* (½ *whole wheat flour is good*)
4 *teaspoons baking powder*
1 *teaspoon salt*
½ *cup water*
   fat for semi-deep frying

Combine dry ingredients. Add water gradually with one hand while working the mixture into a soft dough with the other. More water may be necessary, depending on the barometer reading. Form the dough into two or three balls. Flour hands and clap dough out to a pancake about 6 to 8 inches in diameter. Drop into hot fat and fry quickly until it is crisp and brown on both sides. Drain and serve while still hot.

SCOTCH OATCAKES   ℭ 8

1 *cup sifted flour*	1¾ *cups rolled oats*
1 *tablespoon sugar*	¼ *cup wheat germ*
1 *teaspoon baking powder*	⅓ *cup shortening*
½ *teaspoon salt*	½ *cup milk*

Sift flour, sugar, baking powder, and salt. Relying again on hands, not spoons, blend in oatmeal, wheat germ, and shortening. (Butter-lovers or those not too short of funds might prefer to use some or all butter here.) Pour in milk and mix until sticky. Do this also with the hands; it's easier and, besides, oatmeal and milk are great for the skin. Divide dough into eight balls and roll fairly thin on a floured board. Cut each round part way through into wedges. Bake at 375° for 15 to 20 minutes or until crisp and light brown.

A Yeast Bread for Busy Poets

Most yeast breads result in a floury kitchen and considerable time consumed. A large bowl of rising dough is a bed adored by kittens. Contrarily, this yeast bread requires only one bowl and a baking pan. It requires very little watching. And a cardboard carton turned over the rising dough will foil the most charming kitten.

1 *pound whole wheat flour*
1 *package dry yeast*
1 *tablespoon sugar*
1 *teaspoon salt*
  warm water

Mix flour, salt, and sugar in a large bowl and make a well in the center. Into this pour the yeast that has been dissolved in about 2 tablespoons of warm water. Then add 1½ cups warm water and stir well with the best wooden spoon. The mixture should be soft and sticky. Pour the dough into a *well*-greased bread pan, cover with a cloth, and set in a warm place to rise for about 20 minutes. The dough should come just to the top of the pan. Bake at 425° for approximately 1 hour. A good test for doneness is to thump the bottom of the loaf; it should sound hollow.

This is a heavy, moist loaf, and those with more delicate tastes might prefer using half white flour.

Breadloaves

One nice use for bread is sandwiches. Fail to be limited to the usual and ponder the breadloaf.

Almost anything that is good between two slices of bread is better in a breadloaf. Except peanut butter, perhaps.

The loaf itself, scooped out, makes a dish. It is filled with a combination of ingredients and the bottom crust is refitted as a lid. Wrapped in foil or brown paper, the whole is either baked or well chilled; and when it comes to the table is devoured—dish and all.

French bread, a milk loaf, or almost any bread with a crisp crust can be used. Whatever the choice, the loaf must be unsliced. And however the bread is stuffed it is first prepared as follows: turn the loaf upside down and cut through the bottom crust, leaving about an inch around the edges. Remove the crust in one piece and scoop out the inside. Allow the inside of the shell to dry a little so that the filling will not soak through.

Breadloaves are superior for picnics and covered dish dinners. For, still encased in their foil coats, they are bundled in several layers of newspaper, and will stay either hot or cold for hours. Then, at the end of the day, there's no plate to retrieve, no dirty dish to wash.

Each breadloaf will serve four to six generously.

EAST SIDER

1 *loaf dark rye bread*
1 *pint cottage cheese*
½ *pint sour cream*
  butter

Scoop out the loaf and generously butter the inside. Mix cottage cheese and sour cream with the crumbs that have been taken out of the loaf. Stuff and replace lid. Wrap in foil and refrigerate for an hour or two.

RAINY FRIDAY SPECIAL

1 *round loaf French bread*
1 *pint cottage cheese*
½ *pint sour cream*
1 *teaspoon salt*
2 *eggs*
1 *clove garlic*
  olive oil

Scoop out the loaf and smear the inside with mashed garlic and lots of olive oil. Beat the eggs and combine with the cheese, sour cream, and salt. Fold in about 1½ cups of the bread crumbs. Pour this filling into the loaf, replace the cover, and wrap in foil or brown paper. Bake for 1¼ hours at 350°.

BREADLOAF BEANS

1 *round loaf French bread*
2 *one-pound cans baked beans (or chili beans, etc.)*
  butter

Scoop out the loaf and butter the insides. Heat the beans and drain off as much of the liquid as possible. Stuff the loaf with the beans and a handful of crumbs. Replace cover, wrap in brown paper, and bake for 15 minutes at 425°.

A PICNIC LOAF

1 *round loaf French bread*
4 *tomatoes*
1 *bunch green onions*
1 *3-ounce can chopped ripe olives*
1 *3-ounce jar pimiento-stuffed olives*
2 *tablespoons capers*
2 *tablespoons paprika*
  salt and pepper
  olive oil

Scoop out the loaf and smear the inside with 3 or 4 tablespoons olive oil. Chop the tomatoes and onions. Drain and slice the pimiento-stuffed olives. Combine all the ingredients with enough crumbs to fill the loaf. Replace the lid, wrap in foil, and store in the refrigerator overnight. Wrap the loaf and a chilled bottle of good white wine in several layers of newspaper and be off to the woods.

BREADLOAF BARBECUE

1 *round loaf French or milk bread*
1½ *pounds ground beef*
½ *cup bread crumbs*
½ *cup chili sauce*
1 *teaspoon Worcestershire sauce*
1 *teaspoon vinegar*
1 *teaspoon chili powder*
1 *tablespoon horse-radish*
¼ *cup chopped onions*
1 *clove garlic*
1 *teaspoon salt*
pepper
fat or oil

Scoop out the loaf and set aside. Combine all the other ingredients. Brown in some hot fat, stirring so that the mixture is crumbly. Drain excess fat from time to time. When the meat is almost done drain fat finally and well and stuff the meat into the loaf. Wrap in brown paper and bake 15 minutes at 425°.

SUNDAY-IN-THE-PARK LOAF

Chicken is for Sunday, so here's a breadloaf to fit the weather. Plan for a sunny day, and a cold loaf. But if a cool breeze is forecast, dash the loaf into the oven and pack along a steaming repast.

1 *round loaf French bread*
2 *cups diced cooked chicken*
1 *cup dry white wine*
1 *cup coarsely chopped walnuts*
1 *cup diced celery*
¼ *cup chopped pimiento*
2 *tablespoons chopped onions*
3 *tablespoons chopped parsley*
½ *cup mayonnaise*
½ *cup sour cream or yogurt*
1 *teaspoon lemon juice*
2 *dashes Tabasco*
salt and pepper
butter

Marinate the chicken in wine for several hours and drain well. Mix with all the remaining ingredients.

For a hot day : Scoop out and butter the loaf and stuff with the chicken mixture and perhaps a handful of cherry tomatoes and pitted ripe olives. Replace the lid, wrap the loaf in foil, and chill well.

If a cloud comes over : Heat the chicken mixture in the top part of a double boiler and stuff into a well-buttered loaf. Replace lid, wrap in brown paper, and bake for 15 to 20 minutes at 425°.

OYSTER LOAF

San Franciscans claim this dish as their own. Natives of New Orleans defend their right to ownership. Wherever the origin, the *why* remains the same : Errant husbands would buy small oyster loaves, hurry them home to their wives who would be so delighted with the treat they would fail to scold.

Poor Poets who wander might take note.

1 *round loaf milk bread*	*butter*
2 *dozen medium oysters*	*salt and pepper*
2 *eggs*	2 *or 3 lemons*
cracker crumbs	

Oysters must not be overcooked, so line up everything and plan to work fast.

Scoop out and butter the loaf. It can sit in the oven while the oysters are frying. Melt lots of butter in a heavy pan. Beat the eggs, and set next to them a bowl of cracker crumbs. Dip each oyster into the egg, then the crumbs, and fry quickly to a rich brown. As the oysters are done, place them in the loaf. Sprinkle with salt and pepper, replace lid, and wrap the loaf in brown paper. Bake in a hot oven (425°) for 15 minutes. Serve immediately with lemon wedges, a green salad, and white wine.

DESSERTS

Many *always* end a meal with dessert. Others would *never* think of such a thing, more often announcing this with the implication that the former are a boorish lot. (There are also those who eat desserts all the time and very little else, but they don't count.)

The Poor Poet may be cognizant of the fact that each spoonful of sugar or honey that is part of his dessert will be energy to use for creating, composing, constructing.

Desserts are especially necessary to save an end-of-the-month-type meal. They can be elegant though miniscule: two or three preserved figs and a spoonful of yogurt offered on a doll's plate. They can be simple though enormous, served in soup bowls to celebrate spring: warm homemade shortcake, split and buttered, filled and topped with all the first strawberries the bowl will contain, and honestly running over with whipped cream.

Fruits—In Season and Out

A tray of fresh fruits in summer or a bowl of dried fruits and nuts in winter, with a few leaves or stray flowers tucked in, is centerpiece now—dessert later.

(A similar still life, only smaller, belongs on the writer's desk, near the painter's easel, or close at hand, no matter what the craft.)

Then, too, there are desserts to compound from fruits and assorted additives.

APPLES DEMIJOHN   ℧ 6

6 *cooking apples*
¾ *cup sugar*
1 *cup sweet white wine*
6 *tablespoons apricot jam*
1 *or 2 jiggers brandy*

Core the apples and place in a buttered baking dish. Simmer sugar and wine together for 5 minutes; pour over apples. Cover and bake for 30 to 40 minutes in a 400° oven, or until apples are tender. Drain the syrup from the apples and thicken with the jam and brandy. Pour the syrup over the apples and serve either warm or chilled, plain or with cream.

APPLES IN BOURBON   ℧ 4

A chameleon-sort of dish, Apples in Bourbon is good as an accompaniment to ham or turkey; done in a chafing dish and served plain or with vanilla ice cream, it becomes dessert. And anything that is left over can be used next morning to top a bowl of hot oatmeal.

4 *cooking apples*
6 *tablespoons sugar*
   strips of rind and juice from ½ *lemon*
1 *inch stick cinnamon*
½ *cup bourbon*

Peel and core the apples, leaving them whole or cutting into thick slices. Combine the other ingredients and bring to a boil. Care and a low flame are necessary at this point or else the syrup will burn or ignite, or both. Place the apples in the syrup, cover, and let simmer for 15 to 30 minutes, or until the apples are just tender.

RUMRUNNER BANANAS ♋ 4

This, too, can be dessert or meat accompaniment.

4 *not-too-ripe bananas*
2 *tablespoons butter*
4 *tablespoons brown sugar*

cinnamon
$\frac{1}{4}$ *cup rum*

Melt butter in a frying pan or chafing dish and place in it bananas that have been peeled and sliced in half lengthwise. Sprinkle the bananas with half the brown sugar and a dash of cinnamon and fry until they are lightly browned. Turn and repeat the process. When the bananas are just soft, pour over the rum, ignite, and serve on the spot.

WINEMAKER FIGS ♋ 4

$\frac{1}{2}$ *pound dried figs*
$\frac{1}{4}$ *cup chopped toasted almonds*
1 *tablespoon honey*
$\frac{1}{2}$ *cup port or claret*
1 *teaspoon lemon juice*

Plump the figs by steaming them in a strainer over boiling water. Mix the honey and nuts and stuff each fig. Place figs in a shallow baking dish, pour over the

wine and lemon juice, and heat thoroughly in a 350°
oven, basting occasionally.

Or heat the wine and lemon juice in a chafing dish,
add figs, cover and cook about 10 minutes. In either case,
serve hot with whipped cream flavored with a drop of
almond extract.

GRAPES WITH SOUR CREAM   ∾ 4

1 *pound seedless grapes*
1 *teaspoon lemon juice*
¼ *cup honey*
2 *tablespoons brandy*
1 *pint sour cream*

Combine the lemon juice, honey, and brandy and
pour over the grapes that have been rinsed and stemmed.
Cover and chill overnight. When ready to serve, push
the grapes to one side of the bowl with a large spoon.
Fill the other half with sour cream.

PLUGGED MELON   ∾ 6–8

1 *large honeydew, cantaloupe, or casaba*
1 *to* 1½ *cups Madeira or white dessert wine*

Cut a circular plug from the stem end of the melon
and scoop out the seeds. Fill the melon with wine, replace
the plug, and seal with butter or masking tape. Chill the
melon for at least 2 hours (overnight is better). Serve
spoonfuls of fruit with the wine ladled over.

Or—when the melon is seeded, scoop out the pulp
and mix with any fresh fruits at hand. Stuff the melon
and proceed as above.

And, in either case, consider the possibilities of
Plugged Melon for a late breakfast or a picnic in the
park.

ORANGES WITH BROWN SUGAR AND RUM   ℃ 6

4 *large oranges*   ½ *cup rum*
½ *cup brown sugar*   *orange flower water*

Peel and slice the oranges and allow to chill well. In the meantime, chop the peel and place in a saucepan with the sugar, rum to cover, and any juice from peeling fruit. Heat the sauce to simmer, turn off heat, and allow to stand for at least 2 hours, covered. About an hour before serving, strain the syrup over the oranges, add a dash or two of orange flower water, and stir once. Present in goblets or white porcelain bowls.

CARAMEL PEACHES   ℃ 6

6 *peaches*   1 *cup brown sugar*
1 *tablespoon butter*   ¼ *cup cream*
                       nutmeg

Peel the peaches, leave whole, and place in a heavy frying pan in which butter is melting. Sprinkle sugar over the fruit and simmer, uncovered, for 30 minutes. Turn and baste the peaches every so often. Just before serving, pour cream over and bring just to a boil. Grate a little nutmeg over each serving.

SNOWBOUND PEACHES   ℃ 4

8 *canned peach halves*   ½ *cup currant jelly*
1 *tablespoon cornstarch*   1 *tablespoon lemon juice*
⅓ *cup sugar*   1 *tablespoon butter*
   dash of salt   ¼ *teaspoon cinnamon*
½ *cup Burgundy*   ⅓ *cup shredded coconut*
½ *cup syrup from peaches*

Place drained peaches, cut side up, in a buttered baking dish. Combine the cornstarch, sugar, and salt in a saucepan; add the wine and peach syrup. Stir until smooth and then add the jelly. Bring slowly to a boil, stirring constantly. Continue cooking and stirring until the sauce is thickened and clear—2 or 3 minutes. Remove from heat; add lemon juice, butter, and cinnamon. Pour the sauce over the peaches and sprinkle with coconut.

Bake for 30 minutes at 350° and serve warm to snowbound poets.

CRANBERRY PEARS   ↄ 3–6

6 *pears*
1 *can strained cranberry sauce*
$\frac{1}{2}$ *can water*
2 *jiggers brandy*
   thick cream

Peel, halve, and core the pears. Melt the cranberry sauce and water over low heat and simmer the pears in this syrup until they are just tender. When cool, stir in the brandy, but don't stir so violently that the pears are broken. Serve with thick cream to three or four.

Cranberry Pears, without the cream, is a fine accompaniment to roast turkey or pork. In this case, six may be served.

AMBROSIA

True ambrosia is not dressed up with marshmallows or maraschino cherries or like trappings. It is clean, sharp, and pure, and so desired by Poor Poets—others, too.

Make Ambrosia by cutting up equal parts of oranges and pineapple (preferably fresh), sprinkled with a little sugar and a handful of grated coconut (also preferably fresh). Cover and let chill overnight.

This is excellent as dessert after a big Christmas dinner.

KOSCHAFF

1 *pound dried prunes*
1 *pound dried figs*
$\frac{1}{2}$ *pound dried apricots*
$\frac{1}{2}$ *pound raisins*
$\frac{1}{4}$ *pound blanched almonds or pine nuts*
1 *or 2 lemons*

Soak the prunes overnight, then simmer with the lemons that have been sliced paper-thin. When the prunes are almost tender add the remaining fruits and nuts, remove from the fire, cover, and let chill for at least another day. Serve as is or with a bowl of yogurt on the side.

Koschaff keeps for days and days in the refrigerator.

Cookies

These are the reasons for baking cookies: It is fun. It makes the kitchen smell good. It results in a tin of little desserts. It gives time for contemplation—and an excuse for pinching a sample from each pan.

Even the Poor Poet with only a hot plate for stove can make cookies, though his repertoire may be limited.

HOTPLATE CURRANT BARS ～ 4 dozen

2 *cups sifted cake flour*
1 *teaspoon baking powder*
$\frac{1}{4}$ *teaspoon salt*
$1\frac{1}{2}$ *cups sugar*
3 *tablespoons butter*

1 *teaspoon grated lemon rind*
$\frac{3}{4}$ *cup currants*
1 *egg*
milk

Sift the flour with the other dry ingredients and cut in the butter. Add lemon rind, currants, the egg slightly beaten, and a splash of milk. The dough must be on the dry side, yet held together. Plunk the dough onto a floured board and roll quite thin. (A wine bottle works fine here.) Now cut small bars, diamonds, or fancier shapes. Bake slowly on a buttered griddle, browning each side neatly.

SKILLET OATCAKES   ℧ 2 dozen

Appended to this recipe, and in a fine Spencerian hand, was the notation: "These cakes will not absorb any fat, are very nice and not pernicious." What the writer failed to add was that care must be taken in frying, for the cakes will spread out amazingly and the thin edges must be cautiously pushed toward the middle.

3 *tablespoons each granulated and brown sugar*
1 *teaspoon butter*
3 *teaspoons water*
2 *tablespoons rolled oats*
⅓ *cup finely chopped nut meats*
½ *teaspoon cinnamon*
2½ *tablespoons flour*
   butter for frying

Cream sugar and butter, then stir in the remaining ingredients, one by one, and in the order given. Drop by skimpy teaspoonfuls onto a well-buttered griddle and fry slowly until caramelized and brown on one side; turn and brown the other. Cool on waxed paper.

POET WAFERS   ℧ 3 dozen

3 *eggs*   ½ *cup water*
½ *cup sugar*   ½ *cup melted butter*
½ *teaspoon vanilla*   1 *cup flour*

Beat eggs and sugar well, blend in vanilla and water, and the melted butter and flour alternately. Butter a griddle and bake the cookies one at a time (use a table-spoon of batter for each) for about 1½ minutes on each side. Roll cookies around the handle of a wooden spoon while they're still warm. These may be eaten as they are or filled with whipped cream.

RUM BALLS   ৩ 3½–4 dozen

These don't call for any sort of stove at all—just patience.

> 3 cups crushed vanilla wafers (¼-pound package)
> 1 cup confectioners' sugar
> 3 tablespoons powdered cocoa
> 1 cup finely chopped walnuts or pecans
> 3 tablespoons corn syrup
> ¼ to ½ cup rum

Dump all the ingredients into a bowl and, using hands, mix well. Pinch out small pieces and roll into balls. Roll these in additional confectioners' sugar, pack in a jar with a good tight lid, and allow to age for several weeks, at least.

When the Poor Poet has a kitchen with an oven and a breadboard and a rolling pin he is very lucky indeed. For then, when the muse won't come and the paper in the typewriter is as pristine as an hour ago, it is perhaps time to make cookies. Especially the rolled and cut kind. There is a therapeutic something about rolling the dough, cutting designs, and contemplating the view while waiting for each batch to bake . . . and, perchance, the muse to return.

CARDAMOM COOKIES ℃ 8 dozen

The bon vivant of Scandinavia chews cardamom seeds as a breath sweetener. Ground and made into cookies, the seeds loose a share of their cleansing effect. However, these cookies are exceedingly refreshing, as well as quite crisp.

⅓ cup shortening
1 cup sugar
1 egg
¼ cup milk
2 teaspoons lemon juice
1 tablespoon grated lemon
  rind

2 cups sifted flour
2 teaspoons baking powder
½ teaspoon salt
1½ teaspoons ground
  cardamom

Beat together the shortening, sugar, and egg. Add milk, lemon juice, and rind and mix well. Sift together the dry ingredients and stir the dough thoroughly. Chill and roll a small quantity at a time on a floured board. Cut with a round cookie cutter, place on an ungreased pan and bake for about 5 minutes at 400°.

ANISE RUSKS ℃ 3 dozen

2 large eggs
½ cup plus 2 tablespoons sugar
1¼ cups flour
1 tablespoon anise seeds
1 teaspoon olive oil

Beat the eggs and sugar for 10 minutes. Sift flour and blend thoroughly (gently, though) into the egg-sugar mixture. Stir in anise seeds and oil. Pour into a well-buttered and floured 8-inch-square pan. Bake at 375° for 20 minutes or until the cake is done.

Turn cake out of pan and slice in half and then crosswise in ½ inch slices. Place slices on a well-buttered cookie sheet and return them to the oven. Allow to brown on one side for about 5 minutes, then turn and brown on the other.

Stored in an air-tight tin, Anise Rusks keep for a week or two.

POPPY SEED COOKIES   ҂ 8 dozen

4 *eggs*
1 *cup sugar*
$\frac{1}{2}$ *cup salad oil*
1 *tablespoon grated*
   lemon rind
1 *tablespoon lemon juice*
1 *teaspoon vanilla*

$\frac{1}{4}$ *cup poppy seeds*
$4\frac{1}{2}$ *cups flour*
$1\frac{1}{2}$ *teaspoons baking*
   powder
$\frac{1}{2}$ *teaspoon salt*
cinnamon

Beat the eggs well, then slowly beat in the next six ingredients. Sift 2 cups flour with the other dry ingredients and add to the batter. Now stir in enough additional flour to make a stiff dough. Roll thin on a floured board, cut, sprinkle with a little sugar and cinnamon, and bake at 350° for about 8 minutes.

PFEFFERNÜSSE   ҂ $3\frac{1}{2}$ dozen

A good Christmas tradition not to be overlooked by Poor Poets.

$2\frac{1}{2}$ *cups flour*
$\frac{1}{2}$ *teaspoon each cloves, nutmeg, and cinnamon*
$\frac{1}{4}$ *teaspoon each ginger, black pepper, cardamom,*
   and baking soda
2 *eggs*
1 *cup dark brown sugar, firmly packed*
$\frac{1}{3}$ *cup finely chopped walnuts*

Beat eggs and sugar for 5 minutes. Sift together and add the dry ingredients. Stir in the chopped nuts. Roll cookies the size of large marbles in wet hands. Bake on a greased cookie sheet for 12 to 15 minutes at 375°.

Now, when all the Pfeffernüsse are baked, whip up the following glaze :

½ cup water
1½ cups sugar
   dash cream of tartar
1 egg white

Boil the water, sugar, and cream of tartar to 235° and pour over the stiffly beaten egg white—beating wildly at the same time. Drop the Pfeffernüsse into the glaze, stir to coat, and then remove to a rack to dry.

MORAVIAN COOKIES   ଘ 8 dozen

These are good at Christmas, or any time when the weather is brisk.

¼ cup butter
½ cup molasses
3 tablespoons brown sugar, packed
   a scant ½ teaspoon each ginger, cloves, and
   cinnamon
⅛ teaspoon each nutmeg and allspice
   a dash each salt and black pepper
   a scant ½ teaspoon soda
1⅞ cups sifted cake flour

Heat the molasses and stir in the butter. Add sugar, spices, and soda. Stir in the flour and beat well. Cover the dough and let it stand in a cool place for a week or more. Roll the dough paper-thin, cut, and bake at 375° for about 6 minutes.

ANISPLATZCHEN ℃ 7 dozen

When the gods are with the Poor Poet his Anis-
platzchen will turn out like little mushroom caps: a
crisp bottom, a bit of air space, and a meringue on top.
Much depends on the temperature of the eggs, the length
of beating (grandmother said at least an hour and a half
with a big wooden spoon), and the barometer reading.

> 3 *eggs*
> 1 *cup plus* 1 *tablespoon sugar*
> 1¾ *cups sifted flour*
> ¾ *teaspoon baking powder*
> ½ *teaspoon salt*
> 1½ *tablespoons anise seeds*

The eggs must be at room temperature or a little
better. Using an electric mixer, beat them for 10 minutes. Add sugar gradually, beating constantly, and continue for another half hour. Now add the sifted dry
ingredients and anise and beat for an additional 5
minutes. Drop heaping teaspoonfuls of batter well
apart on a buttered and floured tin. Let the batter dry
for 12 hours. Bake for about 10 minutes at 325° or until
the cakes have puffed and the bottoms are golden. Store
in air-tight tins.

LECKERLEIN ℃ 12 dozen plus

These are definitely *not* for the impatient taste-tester.
For the dough is made one day, stored in a crock, and
all but forgotten for six months to a year. Then, another
day is chosen and the cookies are baked and frosted.
Now they are stacked into a tin between layers of waxed
paper and topped with a cloth generously drenched with
rum. The tin is sealed and hidden away for a year—
perhaps two. Once in a while the seal is broken and more
rum is added, and at these times it is permissible to taste.

Poor Poets who developed a passion for Leckerlein are advised to set up an annual routine so that once the cycle is begun they must never again have to wait 24 long months for the heady flavor of this exceptional cake.

3 pounds honey
½ cup butter
½ pound almonds
¼ pound citron
2 cups sugar
2 teaspoons each allspice, cinnamon, cloves, mace, and nutmeg

1 tablespoon grated lemon rind
plenty of flour
½ ounce carbonate of powdered ammonia
½ cup rum

Heat the honey and melt the butter in it. Stir in the almonds that have been blanched and chopped fine, and chopped citron, and the sugar. Now add the spices and lemon rind. Sift flour and begin stirring it in, adding and stirring until the dough is so stiff that there is some difficulty getting the spoon through it. Dissolve the carbonate of ammonia (available from a druggist) in rum and finally stir this into the dough. Cover and store for at least 6 months.

When baking time arrives, pat the dough into well-greased pans to about ¼ inch thick and bake at 350°. Cut the cake into squares and ice with confectioners' sugar that has been melted with a little water and lemon juice in the top part of a double boiler. Store the cookies as directed above and wait . . .

Desserts from Another Time and Place

As a gala ending to a gala feast, fancy a cluster of desserts that Grandmother considered everyday fare.

For some not too clear reason—packaged foods, perhaps—the wonderful desserts have all but disappeared from the table. The Poor Poet, however, should consider them not as an extravagance (although they really are) but rather as an exercise in true creativity.

PANETTONE
ᘉ 8–10

The Guardian reported, "After a brief struggle with two bank clerks at Swindon, yesterday, three masked raiders escaped in a car with several bags belonging to the clerks." Following a description of both raid and escape, the story concluded, "The bags they stole contained the clerks' lunch."

It is hoped, for the sake of the raiders, that at least one lunch bag contained a generous slab of Panettone. It's a cake that keeps well and could be expected to survive a bank robbery.

½ cup shortening
½ cup butter
1 cup sugar
2 teaspoons almond
    flavoring
1 teaspoon rum flavoring
    or vanilla
3 eggs

3 cups flour
3 teaspoons baking powder
½ teaspoon salt
1¼ cups milk
½ cup each chopped
    walnuts, raisins, and
    glacéd fruit

Cream together the butter, shortening, and sugar. Add the almond and rum flavorings. Beat the eggs well and then beat them into the creamed mixture. Sift together the dry ingredients and blend them alternately with the milk into the creamed mixture. Last, fold in the nuts and fruits.

Pour into a greased and floured angel food cake pan and bake at 350° for one and a half hours, then reduce the heat to 250° and bake an additional 15 minutes. Turn the cake out onto a rack to cool.

BREAD PUDDING ‍ 6

3 *slices toast*
½ *cup raisins*
½ *cup chopped candied fruit*
3 *eggs*
⅓ *cup sugar*
½ *teaspoon salt*
1 *teaspoon grated lemon rind*
1 *teaspoon vanilla*
¼ *teaspoon almond extract*
2 *cups* rich *milk*

Cube the toast and place in a buttered baking dish (about 10 × 6 × 2) and sprinkle with the fruits. Separate one egg, reserve the white, and beat the yolk with the other two eggs. Scald the milk and add it gradually to the eggs, along with the other ingredients. Keep up the beating process. Pour the egg-milk mixture over the bread and fruits, and bake at 350° for 25 minutes or until custard is set. Beat the egg white stiff, fold in 2 tablespoons sugar and swirl on top of the pudding. Bake until the meringue is golden. Serve warm or at room temperature.

CASSATA   ↻ 8–10

   not-too-fresh sponge cake
1 *pound Ricotta cheese*
1½ *cups sugar*
¼ *teaspoon salt*
¼ *cup grated semi-sweet chocolate*
3 *tablespoons chopped candied fruit*
3 *tablespoons rum or orange flower water*

Slice the sponge cake an inch thick and line a spring mold. Beat all the other ingredients and pour into the mold. Top with additional slices of cake that have been crumbled. Refrigerate overnight and when ready to serve remove the cake from the mold and dust with powdered sugar and a few sliced blanched almonds, if they're available.

FLOATING ISLAND   ↻ 6–8

There is absolutely nothing so nice on a summer day as a big crystal bowl full of Floating Island.
For the custard :

   2 *cups milk*
3 *egg yolks*
½ *teaspoon vanilla*
¼ *cup sugar*
⅛ *teaspoon salt*

Scald the milk in a double boiler. Beat the egg yolks with the sugar. Slowly add the hot milk to the yolks, stirring constantly. Return the mixture to the double boiler and continue stirring and cooking until the custard thickens and a thin coating is formed on the spoon. Add salt and vanilla and pour into a serving dish. For the islands:

3 *egg whites*
3 *tablespoons powdered sugar*
1 *teaspoon vanilla*

Beat the whites until stiff, then gradually add the sugar and vanilla. Place by spoonfuls on hot, not boiling, water and cover. Test in a few minutes by running a knife through an island. If the knife comes out clean the islands are done. Place them on the custard and chill well.

RUMOS TORTE   ᘓ 8–10

¾ *cup sugar*
¾ *cup water*
¼ *cup rum*
½ *teaspoon vanilla*
3 *sponge cake layers*

¼ *cup raspberry jam*
¼ *cup ground almonds*
    rum-flavored whipped
    cream

Combine the sugar and water and boil for 5 minutes. Add rum and vanilla and one of the sponge cake layers, crumbled. Spread half the jam on the second sponge cake layer and top with the rum-soaked crumbs, the almonds, and the third sponge cake layer which has also been spread with jam. The jam side goes down, this time. Weight the cake with a flat plate and let stand overnight. Serve doused with whipped cream that has been generously spiked with additional rum.

CHEESE CAKE   ᘓ 8–10

The cheese cake fancier, haunted by repeated failure, might be put in better mental state to know that there is at least *one* foolproof formula.

graham cracker crumb crust for an 8-inch pan
½ pound cream cheese
1 large egg
6 tablespoons sugar
½ teaspoon grated lemon rind
1 teaspoon orange flower water
½ cup sour cream
1 tablespoon sugar
  a few drops vanilla
  salt

Cream together the creamed cheese, egg, 6 tablespoons sugar, lemon rind, orange flower water, and a dash of salt, and pour the mixture into an 8-inch pie pan lined with graham cracker crust. Top this with the sour cream that has been mixed with a tablespoon of sugar and the vanilla. Bake in a 350° oven for 8 minutes. Cool, and chill before serving. This is quite rich, and goes a long long way.

FRIED CREAM   ♋ 12

3 egg yolks
1 jigger rum
¼ cup sugar
  pinch salt
3 tablespoons cornstarch
2 cups cream

1 inch vanilla bean
  grating of nutmeg
  cracker crumbs
1 egg
  butter
¼ cup rum

Beat together the egg yolks, jigger of rum, sugar, and salt. Make a paste of the cornstarch and an equal part of water or milk and add to the egg yolk mixture. Heat the cream with the vanilla bean and nutmeg and gradually stir this into the yolks. Cook and stir in a double boiler until the custard is quite thick and smooth. Remove the vanilla bean, rinse it, and save it for another day. Pour the cream into a buttered shallow pan and chill.

When ready to serve, cut the cream into small rectangles and dip in crumbs, then in a slightly beaten egg, and once again in crumbs. Fry in butter or hot deep fat, place on a warm serving plate, slosh with ¼ cup warm rum, and ignite.

A rich dessert that calls for tiny cups of strong Italian coffee.

WHISKEY PUDDING   ભ 12

This is almost too elegant.

½ *pound lady fingers*
½ *cup ground almonds*
¼ *cup sliced maraschino cherries*
8 *eggs*
2 *cups bourbon*
¾ *cup sugar*
   dash of almond or vanilla extract
   salt

Line a large serving dish (crystal is preferred) with split lady fingers and cherries and sprinkle in half the almonds. Separate the eggs and beat the yolks with two tablespoons sugar until they are light. Warm the bourbon in the top of a double boiler and carefully stir it into the yolks. Cook the custard over hot water until it is quite thick, then pour it into the lady-finger-lined dish.

Beat the egg whites until stiff and fold in the remaining sugar, a dash of salt, and the almond extract. Spread on top of the custard, sprinkle with the rest of the almonds, and bake in a 325° oven until the meringue is golden.

If the best crystal serving dish was used, bake the meringue on a cookie sheet and then transfer it to the custard.

Whiskey Pudding is to be served cold.

SCRIPTURE CAKE

A recipe to be read rather than followed.

1 *cup butter*, JUDGES, 5:25
3½ *cups flour*, I. KINGS, 4:22
2 *cups sugar*, JER. 6:20
2 *cups raisins*, I. SAM. 30:12
2 *cups figs*, I. SAM. 30:12
1 *cup water*, GEN. 24:17
1 *cup almonds*, GEN. 43:11
   little salt, LEV. 2:13
6 *eggs*, IS. 10:14
   sweet spices to taste, I. KINGS, 10:2
1 *tablespoonful honey*, EX. 16:31

Follow Solomon's advice for making good boys and you will have a good cake, PROV. 23:14. Sift 2 teaspoonfuls of baking powder with flour, blanch the almonds, chop figs.

GILDING THE LILY

Calm anticipation of the unexpected dinner guest: a virtue of necessity for Poor Poets—and others.

A freezer stuffed with roasts, chops, stews, vegetables, soups, and pies leads to this state. So does the corner delicatessen. So, too, does a shelf of comestibles designed solely for gilding the lily.

But the gilt must be as pure and good as Mrs. March's popovers or the treats that Ratty packed into his picnic basket.

A supper of baked beans, corn bread with butter, and cole slaw, though not remarkable, is satisfying. Embellish the same menu with a tray holding many little crocks of relishes and supper becomes a feast. And—takes care of the unexpected guest.

In this category cottage cheese goes well with eggs, baked beans, or ham. It can be tossed with almost any salad. It can be folded into buttered noodles. It can be mixed with candied or dried fruits, jam or jelly, deviled meats, anchovies, or herbs for sandwiches, dips, or décor.

Sour cream or plain yogurt belongs in a big bowl next to potatoes or pilaf, peas, green beans, and eggplant. Or fruit compote.

These, along with celery, carrots, green onions, and radishes, refrigerator staples to most: to the inventive, items that not only gild the lily but recall all the treats in art and literature.

Then there are things to make and store on a shelf; insurance against the unexpected.

Relishes from Jars and Tins

MUSTARD OLIVES

¼ cup vinegar
1 tablespoon dry mustard
1 teaspoon mustard seeds
1 #1 can ripe or green-ripe olives
1 tablespoon olive oil

Dump mustard and mustard seeds into a small saucepan and slowly blend in the vinegar, olive oil, and liquid from the canned olives. Bring the mixture to a boil, add olives, and simmer 10 minutes. Cool and refrigerate. Mustard Olives, which should be drained just before serving, improve with several days' aging.

HERB OLIVES

1 cup drained ripe olives
½ cup olive oil
½ bay leaf, crumbled
1 chili pepper, crumbled
1 tablespoon capers

1 clove garlic, mashed
6 rosemary leaves
1 teaspoon celery seeds or
*   several leaves*

Plop everything into a jar with a good lid, shake well, and store in refrigerator for at least 3 days. Reshaking and taste-testing each day is permissible. When the olives have been eaten (by taste-testing?) the oil can be used for salads.

10-DAY STUFFED OLIVES

A good way to extend the life of a jar of opened and aging stuffed olives.

1 *cup stuffed green olives*
½ *teaspoon oregano*
½ *bay leaf, crumbled*
½ *teaspoon paprika*
1 *clove garlic, mashed*
¼ *cup vinegar*
¼ *cup brine from olives*

Drain the olives, reserving ¼ cup brine. Sprinkle herbs, paprika, and garlic over the olives in the jar, and then cover with vinegar and reserved brine. Cover the jar, shake, and store in the refrigerator for at least 10 days, giving the jar further shakes at intervals.

CURRIED PICKLES

⅓ *cup cider vinegar*
⅓ *cup brown sugar, firmly packed*
1 *tablespoon curry powder*
1 *12-ounce jar sliced cucumber pickles, drained*

Combine the vinegar, sugar, and curry powder and simmer for 10 minutes before pouring over the pickles and recapping the jar. Allow the concoction to stand a day or two before serving.

50-MINUTE PEACH BUTTER

1 #2½ can sliced cling   3 tablespoons cider vinegar
  peaches   ½ teaspoon cinnamon
½ cup brown sugar, packed   ⅛ teaspoon ground cloves

Drain peaches and cut coarsely, and combine in a saucepan with all other ingredients. Bring to a boil and simmer 20 minutes, stirring off and on. Sieve or leave in chunks, cool, and refrigerate.

FRUITS IN HONEY AND WINE

Canned peaches, pears, apricots, fruits for salad, or a combination, treated with honey and wine, are a superb side dish with meats or poultry.

1 cup honey
¾ cup cider vinegar
10 whole cloves
1 stick cinnamon
¾ cup port or muscatel wine
1½ quarts well-drained canned fruit (2 #2½ cans)

Combine and simmer for 5 minutes the honey, vinegar, cloves, and cinnamon. Add the wine and fruit and continue to simmer 15 minutes longer. Cool and store in refrigerator.

PICKLED BEETS

1 #303 can sliced beets (about 2 cups)
½ cup juice from beets
6 tablespoons cider vinegar
1 tablespoon sugar
1 scant teaspoon salt
2 teaspoons each cloves and dry mustard
  dash of cinnamon and allspice
1 small clove garlic

Pack drained beets in a quart jar. Mix the other ingredients in a saucepan, bring to a boil, and pour over the beets. Cover, cool, and refrigerate until ready to use. Good with sour cream!

Like the magic pudding, this dish can grow and grow. As the number of beet slices in the jar diminishes, whole hard-cooked eggs, sliced onions, or parboiled celery or carrot sticks can be dropped into the pickling liquid. They should be ready to eat in a day or two.

BEETS WITH HORSE-RADISH

1 #303 *can diced beets*
4 *tablespoons sugar*
6 *tablespoons prepared horse-radish*
6 *tablespoons finely chopped onions*
4 *tablespoons vinegar*
½ *teaspoon salt*
¼ *teaspoon pepper*

Empty the drained beets into a bowl, measure in the other ingredients, stir well, cover, and refrigerate. These should be allowed to stand an hour or so before using. A must with roast beef.

PLUM SAUCE

The Chinese serve Plum Sauce as a dip for egg roll, fried shrimp, barbecued spareribs, roast pork, and roast chicken. It is not to be overlooked.

1 *cup plum jelly*
½ *cup chutney*
1 *tablespoon cider vinegar*
1 *tablespoon sugar*

Blend the four ingredients, let stand several hours, and the sauce is ready.

SAMBAL

This is a Javanese hot (!) sauce that is necessary for Nasi Goreng Rice or Rijstafel. Two-ounce jars of the imported variety are uncommon, even in specialty food shops.

4 *tablespoons raw white fish*
2 *tablespoons brown sugar*
1 *yeast cake*
1 *clove garlic*
½ *cup seeded and chopped red pepper*
½ *cup chopped onion*
½ *teaspoon salt*
¼ *cup or more peanut oil*

Chop the fish and then mix in a mortar with the yeast, garlic, and sugar until the mixture becomes a paste. Cover and let stand for 24 hours.

Grind the peppers, onion, and salt to a paste.

Pour the oil into a heavy pan with lid and fry and stir the fish paste until the fish is cooked. Stir in the vegetable paste (be sure there is sufficient oil), cover and cook over very low heat until the oil has turned red. Makes a generous ½ cup.

A HOT MUSTARD

The tales that mustard seeds have mysterious powers is even more believable when this, or the following mustard, is set on the table.

¼ *cup dry mustard*
2 *tablespoons sugar*
¼ *teaspoon turmeric*
   dash of salt
1 *small clove garlic, mashed*
   cider vinegar
   water

Combine the dry ingredients and garlic. Add sufficient water and vinegar (about half as much vinegar as water) to make a thick cream. Mix well, cover, and let stand about 10 minutes before using. A drop or two of oil will give the mustard a smoother consistency and brighter color. Makes ¼ cup.

BAYOU MUSTARD

¼ *cup dry mustard*
½ *teaspoon sugar*
¼ *teaspoon each salt, thyme, horse-radish, and*
   Tabasco
⅛ *teaspoon pepper*
1 *teaspoon flour*
2 *tablespoons mayonnaise*

Mix the dry ingredients; stir in the Tabasco, horse-radish, and mayonnaise, and enough boiling water to make a thick paste. Cover and let stand a half hour or more before using. Makes ⅓ cup.

Vinegars

WINE VINEGAR

Vinegar, purple in color and definitely tasting like *wine*, that is sometimes found in family-style Italian restaurants, may be manufactured at home. With patience. Equipment consists of an empty wine bottle with cork and a small funnel.

To proceed, pour half a cup or so of good commercial wine vinegar into the bottle. To this add (and continue adding at intervals) leftover red wines. A good wine vinegar should have developed in several months, though it will improve as time goes on. Impatient taste-testers might start several bottles at once so that at least one batch has a good year and a half to mature properly.

HERB VINEGAR

Herbs, either picked fresh from the garden or selected from cartons, lend an exotic caste to wine vinegar.

1 *pint each red and white wine vinegar*
4 *sprigs thyme*
2 *sprigs marjoram or oregano*
1 *sprig each sage, savory, and rosemary*
1 *clove garlic, bruised*
1 *or 2 whole cloves*

Place everything in a jar, cover with a non-corrosive lid, and let stand 2 weeks. The garlic should be removed after the first 24 hours. Strain the vinegar before using.

Alternate amounts if using dried herbs would be 1 teaspoon thyme leaves, $\frac{1}{2}$ teaspoon marjoram or oregano leaves, and $\frac{1}{4}$ teaspoon each sage, savory, and rosemary leaves.

NASTURTIUM VINEGAR

2 *cups green nasturtium seeds*
$\frac{1}{4}$ *cup salt*
2 *cups cider or white wine vinegar*

Fill a quart jar half full of nasturtium seeds, sprinkle with salt, cover, and allow to stand overnight. Next day fill the jar with vinegar, cover with a non-corrosive lid, and let lurk in a dark cupboard to ripen for several weeks.

Seasoning Salts

Develop a customized seasoning salt (or several). It saves, for example, the effort of hauling out half a dozen jars and cartons just to make one deviled egg.

For a start, here's a seasoning salt that's good in pot roasts or stews, and with poultry.

1 *cup salt*
1 *teaspoon pepper*
1 *teaspoon paprika*
½ *teaspoon ground ginger*
½ *teaspoon dry mustard*
½ *teaspoon crushed oregano*
⅓ *teaspoon cayenne*
⅓ *teaspoon mace*
¼ *teaspoon (heaping) garlic powder)*

Mix, and store in a jar with a tight lid.

Jellies

Glasses of jelly from the store, melted, treated with herbs or spices, and allowed to reset . . . a profitable kitchen adventure for a dreary day.

Melt the jelly either in the top part of a double boiler or in a small pan over a low flame. For more flavor, the herbs should be added while the jelly is hot. However, for aesthetic purposes, i.e., a branch or leaf suspended midway in the finished product, this work must be carried on while the jelly is cooling.

Apple jelly takes well to a branch of sweet basil, sage, or mint; leaves of lemon verbena, rose geranium, or nasturtium; a cinnamon stick, or several whole cloves.

Lemon jelly is picked up with the addition of a branch of tarragon, marjoram, rosemary, sage, or thyme.

Grape jelly becomes special when a broken cinnamon stick, several whole cloves, or bruised cardamom seeds are added.

And then there is:

WINE JELLY

1 *package raspberry-flavored gelatin*
¾ *cup boiling water*
¾ *cup sherry*
1 *tablespoon claret*
2 *tablespoons brandy*

Dissolve the gelatin in boiling water and stir in the wines and brandy. Pour into a mold and chill until set.

Yogurt

Because yogurt is a main dish, a side dish, or an ingredient for so many recipes, the Poor Poet would do well to learn to make his own.

Bring 1 quart of milk (whole, skim, canned, or reconstituted dry) just to a boil. Cool to lukewarm and stir in 1 tablespoon commercial yogurt. Cover the container and let stand in a warm place overnight, then chill before using.

Yogurt, mixed half and half with cold water, is a good pick-me-up.

Yogurt, drained overnight or for several days in a cheesecloth-lined colander, may be turned out on a plate, sprinkled with salt, and drenched with olive oil, and used for a spread for crackers or toast. This may be varied with a sprinkling of chopped mint leaves or chopped ripe olives.

POOR POET TRIFLES

Simmer tiny beets in orange juice and serve with their uncooked tops, egg yolk balls, and shredded carrot and onion.

The milk bath was promoted as a publicity stunt. Drinking it proves more beneficial.

Spread toast with butter mixed with toasted sesame seeds and brown under a flame.

Poor Poets—and others—who combine the cocktail hour with cooking should take care that they don't overseason the food.

Sprinkle hot baked apples or pears with grated cheese.

Olives will keep for months if about an inch of olive oil is poured over the olives and their brine and the jar tightly capped.

A new iron kettle may be cleaned by boiling in it a good-sized handful of hay.

Anchovy fillets rolled in nutmeg and chopped mint leaves is a good appetizer.

Ginger poultices, instead of mustard, will relieve neuralgia and will not blister.

Fry tomatoes in pure olive oil and minced garlic and serve with French bread.

Vanilla beans, used to flavor milk or custard, can be washed, dried, and stored for re-use.

Try Danish squash filled with peas, tiny onions, mushrooms, and meat gravy—baked.

Seventeenth-century princes sent each other potatoes as a curiosity.

Tag ends of jam can be brought back to life with a little hot water and brandy.

So can dried fruits that have been allowed to sit on the shelf too long.

Sweep the floor every day and keep a pot of geraniums at the window.

For Sunday breakfast, top oatmeal with brown sugar and a splash of rum. Ignite.

Always buy *fresh* rolls.

And always cook with *butter* !

INDEX